THE
MILLIONAIRE
IN YOU

Also by Michael LeBoeuf

The Perfect Business

Fast Forward

How to Win Customers and Keep Them for Life

The Greatest Management Principle in the World

The Productivity Challenge

Working Smart

THE
MILLIONAIRE
IN YOU

Ten Things You Need to Do
Now to Have Money and the Time
to Enjoy It

MICHAEL LEBOEUF, PH.D.

NEW YORK

Published by Crown Business, New York, New York.
Member of the Crown Publishing Group, a division of Random House, Inc.

www.randomhouse.com

CROWN BUSINESS is a trademark and the Rising Sun colophon is a registered trademark of Random House, Inc.

Printed in the United States of America

Design by Meryl Sussman Levavi/Digitext

Library of Congress Cataloging-in-Publication Data
LeBoeuf, Michael.
    The millionaire in you : ten things you need to do *now* to have money and the time to enjoy it / Michael LeBoeuf.
        p.   cm.
    Includes index.
        1. Finance, Personal.   2. Investments.   3. Success.   I. Title.
    HG179. L412 2002
    332.024—dc21   2001047566

ISBN 0-609-61006-6

10 9 8 7 6 5 4 3 2 1

First Edition

At the end of the twentieth century, one in fourteen U.S. households had a net worth of over $1 million. This book is dedicated to those who read, see and hear all the millionaire hype and ask, "WHERE'S MINE?" May this book help you find it.

CONTENTS

Introduction   1

Part I—SEE IT!

Insight 1   The Time and Wealth Grid   7

Insight 2   LeBoeuf's Law—The Best-Kept Investment
             Secret in the World   12

Insight 3   The Master Key to Wealth   20

Insight 4   The Twentieth Century's Greatest Gift   29

Part II—DO IT!
TEN CHOICES FOR ACHIEVING
PERSONAL AND FINANCIAL FREEDOM

Choice 1   Live the Life You Want Instead of the Life
             Others Expect   37

Choice 2   Stack the Odds in Your Favor Instead of
             Against You   51

Choice 3   Be a Super Saver Instead of a Big Spender   63

Choice 4   Increase the Market Value of Your Time Instead of
            Working Long Hours   79

Choice 5   Do Less Better Instead of Trying to Do It All   92

Choice 6   Capitalize on the Unexpected Instead of Being
            Derailed by It   106

Choice 7   Own the Market Instead of Trying to Beat
            the Market   118

Choice 8   Limit Your Losses Instead of Letting
            Bad Luck Ruin You   136

Choice 9   Listen to Those Who Know Instead
            of Those Who Sell   150

Choice 10   Do It Now Instead of Regretting It Later   164

Part III—CELEBRATE AND ENJOY IT!

Job #1   Stay Financially Independent   177

Job #2   Keep Physically and Mentally Active   183

Job #3   Experience the Joy of Giving Something Back   189

Job #4   Remember, the Journey Is the Joy   197

            The Millionaire in You: Summary   201

            Acknowledgments   203

            Index   205

"Nobody cuts through the confusion and complication like Michael LeBoeuf. In *The Millionaire in You*, he efficiently distills the wisdom of work and money into a volume that isn't just readable but enjoyable. LeBoeuf doesn't just educate, he charms. He takes difficult material and makes it sing and dance. He doesn't present ideas, he choreographs them. *The Millionaire in You* confirms Michael LeBoeuf as the Obiwan Kenobe of business writers, a Wise Counselor whose advice is not just helpful, but wise, steady, warm, and compassionate."

—Dale Dauten, syndicated columnist and author of *The Gifted Boss*

"*The Millionaire in You* is chock-full of common sense, practical ideas, and strategies that really work . . . not the get-rich-quick, wishful thinking type of advice that's all too commonly dished out. I wish I had known LeBoeuf's Law and had a copy of this book when I was starting out. If you are looking for the perfect graduation or wedding gift, *The Millionaire in You* is it!"

—Susan Roane, author of *How to Work a Room* and *What Do I Say Next?*

"An important book at a critical time. When it comes to building financial wealth, Wall Street wants us to tune in to irrelevant stock market summaries, monthly economic numbers, and quarterly earnings reports. Finally, someone has written a masterpiece that gets us to focus on what matters most of all. In his book, *The Millionaire in You,* Michael LeBoeuf shares simple principles that are certain to enrich your financial and emotional well-being forever. Not only does he detail the basics of an intelligent investment plan, but he reveals how you can use your financial resources to accentuate a far greater purpose—the gift of your self in this world."   —Bill Schultheis, author of *The Coffeehouse Investor*

"Michael LeBoeuf has written the bible for people who want to be successful. *The Millionaire in You* should be a required college course for any degree, and I can assure you this is now my standard graduation gift. I really believe this is the first book any graduate should read after college and it should be required reading every three years. In fact, it should also be required reading for a marriage license."

—Donald J. Landry, former CEO of Sunburst Hospitality Corp., Choice Hotels International, Manor Care Hotel Division and Richfield Hotel Management

INTRODUCTION

Father: Wealth and fame do not buy happiness.
Teenage son: Have you ever tried it?

—JIM BERRY

When Michelangelo was asked to describe how he carved his classic work *David* from a block of damaged marble, he replied that the statue was already in the stone. All he did was see it and then chisel away the unnecessary marble to reveal it.

Like the masterpiece inside the marble, there's a potential millionaire and a wonderful life of personal freedom living inside you and every one of us. The key to making it a reality lies in seeing the possibilities and then making the right choices to create it.

There are only four things you need to know about money:

- How to make it
- How to save it
- How to invest it
- How to enjoy it

Very, very few people manage to do all four, although almost anyone can. The answer lies in applying a simple principle that I call LeBoeuf's Law. In the pages that follow, I'm going to teach you that principle and show you how to put it to work.

HAVE I GOT A DEAL FOR YOU

Suppose someone wants to hire you to do a job. You start it on Monday morning and need to complete it by five P.M. on Friday. The job is one you are well qualified for and capable of doing in the allotted time. Your supervisor agrees to pay you a certain amount when the job is satisfactorily completed.

But here's the best part: If you do the job right and finish early, you get to take the rest of the week off and receive a bonus of twenty times the promised payment. There's no catch. Would you like a job like that? Who wouldn't?

Well, I have great news for you. There's a similar offer in your hands right now, and the younger you are, the greater the potential bonus is. It might be forty, sixty or even a hundred times the amount you were promised. There are only two differences between the fantasy offer and the real one. First, the real offer isn't for a week. It's for the rest of your working life. And second, the real person who wants to hire and pay you is you! To put it another way, if you make a commitment to yourself and are willing to do what it takes to become a millionaire, you almost certainly will.

Don't tell me it can't be done, because I've done it, and millions of others have, too. Like the overwhelming majority of today's millionaires, I didn't inherit a dime. I went to public schools and state universities. I had only one full-time job as a university professor, which I started at the late age of twenty-seven and retired from at forty-seven. I didn't begin seriously pursuing my journey to financial freedom until thirty-five. In retrospect, I realize that I could have retired comfortably at forty-three, and in two of my final four years as a professor, I took an unpaid leave of absence.

Was I lucky? You bet I was. I had two good parents, I enjoyed good health and I was lucky to be born in a very rich country where education and wealth are attainable to those who choose to reach for it. I'm a great believer in the old saying that luck happens when opportunity meets preparation.

NO HIDDEN AGENDAS

I wrote this book because I want you to become financially independent and enjoy the same freedom that I do. I have no hidden agendas. I don't want to sell investments, financial services or any kind of business opportunity to anybody. I've made my fortune and earned my freedom, and I intend to keep both. My goal is simply to help as many people as possible become millionaires as quickly, safely, honestly and enjoyably as possible.

The Millionaire in You uses the same three-step process that Michelangelo employed in creating the *David*. First, he visualized the masterpiece in his mind's eye. Then he created it. Finally, he stepped back to celebrate his creation and enjoy it. And those are the same three steps to creating the millionaire in you. First, you see the possibilities. Second, you do what it takes to create your fortune. Finally, you step back, celebrate your financial freedom and enjoy it. See it! Do it! Celebrate and enjoy it!

DOES MONEY BUY HAPPINESS?

This very important question needs answering at the outset, because becoming a millionaire isn't easy. Unless you're born to rich parents, break the law, win the lottery or hit a hot streak at a casino, attaining financial freedom takes years of time, work, sacrifice and self-discipline. Is it worth the effort? We have all heard many times that money can't buy happiness.

If you believe the results of recent investigations into the subject, money indeed does buy happiness. According to a report from HNW Digital of Newton, Massachusetts, a full 86% of the wealthiest 8.6 million Americans ranked financial success and security as important to their overall happiness, and 50% said it was very important. Moreover, 75% of America's wealthiest reported that they have become happier as they have accumulated more money. The people who tell us that money can't buy happiness either don't have it or don't know where to shop.

Economists Jonathan Gardner and Andrew Oswald of England's University of Warwick studied people who inherited or won large sums of money. Not surprisingly, they found that a large windfall is followed by a marked increase in overall happiness the following year. According to the study, coming into an extra $75,000 makes one significantly happier, and a windfall of £1 million (the equivalent of $1.5 million U.S.) will take someone from the bottom to the top of the happiness scale.

Both studies report that happiness isn't affected by how one comes into the money. Winning it, earning it and inheriting it all work equally well. This reminds me of the husband who asked his wife, "Do you love me just because my father left me a fortune?" She replied, "Not at all, honey. I would love you no matter who left you the money."

The famous poet and playwright Oscar Wilde once remarked, "When I was young I thought that money was the most important thing in life; now that I am old I know that it is." My personal opinion is that happiness isn't determined by what you have, it's determined by what you think about what you have. If you think you would enjoy being a millionaire, it's a safe bet you will. So let's stop fantasizing and do something about it. Read on.

Part I

SEE IT!

We have enough youth, how about a fountain of SMART?

—Anonymous

Any American today with basic common sense can become a millionaire. It's simply a matter of seeing the possibilities, knowing how to proceed and following through. Let's begin with four insights. The first, one of two brand-new insights that *The Millionaire in You* teaches, explodes a commonly held belief about the relationship between money and time. It also identifies where you are in your journey to wealth. The second new insight, LeBoeuf's Law, is the grand strategy for getting you from where you are to where you want to be—having money and the time to enjoy it. The third insight points out the master key to wealth and the two most important rules for managing time and money. Finally, we will look at the twentieth century's greatest gift and how you can use it to become richer than you ever imagined.

THE TIME AND WEALTH GRID

"Normal" is getting dressed in clothes that you buy for work, driving through traffic in a car that you are still paying for, in order to get to the job that you need so you can pay for the clothes, car and the house that you leave empty all day in order to afford to live in it.

—ELLEN GOODMAN, SYNDICATED
COLUMNIST

It's the scourge of modern-day living that plagues most of us: If you have the money, you don't have the time. If you have lots of time, you're hurting for money. And most of us could use a whole lot more of both. *Welcome to the time/money trap.*

Just how prevalent is this problem? Take a look for yourself. Visit the jam-packed California freeways, the Long Island Expressway, commuter trains or other urban traffic arteries during rush hour. What you will see is literally millions of people frantically rushing to and from work, where they put in long hours so they can make the payments on a house and a lifestyle that they don't have time to enjoy. It's life on a treadmill.

Want to see how the affluent live? Visit a California or Florida marina and look at all those expensive pleasure boats. What you will notice is that they're empty and docked 99% of the time. And where are all the wanna-be sailors? You know where they are—putting in their time to pay the bills while the empty boats sit tied to the docks.

How do you get out of the time/money trap? First, you have to understand how you got there in the first place. We fall into the trap by thinking with a paycheck mentality. That's a mind-set that views discretionary time and money as two ends of a continuum that look like this:

Discretionary Time $\vdash$————————————$\dashv$ Money

Because most of think with a paycheck mentality, we assume that having more of one requires sacrificing some of the other. But as the title of an old song reminds us, "It ain't necessarily so." Time and money aren't one-dimensional trade-offs unless we assume they are and choose to live our lives that way. Unfortunately, most people do.

Let's replace the paycheck mind-set with a whole new way of looking at time and money that's much more attuned to reality. Take a look at the Time and Wealth Grid.

Each of us is represented at some point on the chart with respect to our amount of wealth and discretionary time. Discretionary time is represented on the horizontal axis on a relative scale from one to ten; net worth is depicted on the vertical axis on a scale from one to ten. Consider the five people depicted on the chart. While all five lead very different lives, all but one is in the time/money trap. Which one is most like you? Where would you place yourself on the grid?

(**1,1,**): The Slave has little or no wealth or discretionary time. She may be a single parent forced to work long hours

WHICH OF THE FOLLOWING TYPES IS MOST LIKE YOU?

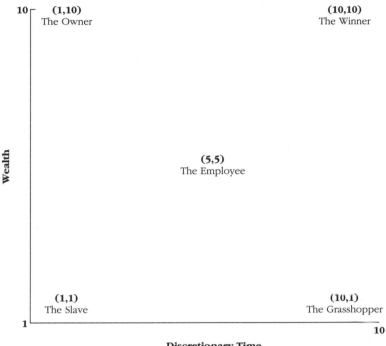

for low pay to make ends meet, or her debts and obligations may be so large that she must work several jobs just to pay the bills.

(**10,1**): The Grasshopper has plenty of time and little or no wealth. Like the grasshopper that appears in the fable with the ant, he spends his days living in the moment with little or no concern for acquiring or saving. He believes in the old saying "You can't take it with you." That's true, but he's not going anywhere without it, either. Unless he wises up, the life of his dreams will remain just that—a dream and nothing more.

(**5,5**): The Employee represents most of us. She works regular hours for a decent living wage that pays the rent and puts food on the table. She trades time for money, and she focuses on earning to spend. Unless that mind-set changes, she will continue to trade time for money for the rest of her working days. Then she will retire and spend her golden years living on a modest pension.

(**1,10**): The Owner has plenty of wealth but little discretionary time. He is usually a well-educated, self-employed professional, corporate executive or entrepreneur whose life is consumed by work. He thinks he owns a business, but in reality, the business owns him; he thinks he has a career, but the career has him. He thinks he owns several expensive homes and toys (such as a yacht or airplane), but they really own him: He has to keep working to maintain them and acquire more. He lives with long hours, high stress, fatigue and strained relationships. It's common for Owners to marry and beget Grasshoppers who squander their fortunes after the Owners are gone.

(**10,10**): The Winner enjoys the best of all possible worlds. The Owner is rich because of what he owns. The Winner is wealthy because he has money *and* the time to enjoy it. The Winner doesn't work for money. His money works for him and creates more than he spends. If he continues to work, as many Winners do, it's because he wants to, not because he has to. He realizes that wealth is only a means to an end and that end is a balanced, productive, enjoyable, fulfilling life. Owners are rich but not free. Winners are rich and free. They live the life of their dreams. As Benjamin Franklin noted, "Wealth is not his that has it, but his that enjoys it."

Most winners didn't inherit their life of privilege. They are no more intelligent, hardworking or lucky than others. They got where they are by learning how to make money and time work for them.

The purpose of this book is to provide you with the insight, the motivation and the tools to get you from wherever you are on the chart to (10,10): the winner's circle. Knowing what's in this book won't make you wealthy—applying what's in it will. If you have the desire, discipline and dedication to become wealthy, I'll teach you what you need to know to make it happen.

LEBOEUF'S LAW—THE BEST-KEPT INVESTMENT SECRET IN THE WORLD

We need education in the obvious more than investigation of the obscure.

—OLIVER WENDELL HOLMES

If you have ever been in any leadership position, ever worked as a manager, military officer, teacher or coach, you know how important strategy is to achieve your goals. I believe it was Napoleon who said that most battles are won or lost long before the first shot is fired. It's the game plan, more than anything else, that dictates outcomes. With an effective strategy, you can be successful even in the face of tactical mistakes. But if your strategy is poor, all the great tactics in the world won't save you. A poor game plan almost always guarantees failure. It's true in war, sports, business and life.

Your journey to the winner's circle begins when you realize that the key to financial freedom is about something far more important and precious than money. Wealth begins when you realize the value of your time and learn how to invest it effectively.

Unlike money, time is irreplaceable. You can't make it or save it. But like money, time can be measured, invested and enjoyed. Let's face it: If you don't enjoy your time, life *will* seem like forever. If you have ever been stuck in a bad relationship or a job you hate, or suffered through a lengthy illness, you know what I mean.

THE GRAND STRATEGY

Believe it or not, I've discovered a single simple principle that will enable you to get a terrific return on your investment of time and money. Like Albert Einstein's formula of $E=MC^2$, it's simple but incredibly powerful. Here it is. Etch it in your brain:

> *LeBoeuf's Law: Invest your time actively and your money passively.*

Actively investing your time means deciding how your time will be spent rather than spending it according to current circumstances or the dictates of others. Begin by taking a look at your life, your dreams, what's most important to you and what you want. Then resolve to spend your time doing what will get you from where you are to where you want to be in a way that's most satisfying to you.

Just as a financial portfolio allocates dollars among various types of investments such as stocks, bonds and cash, you have to decide how to allocate your portfolio of time. A good time portfolio invests waking hours in four basic activities:

- Learning
- Earning
- Living
- Giving

How much time we allocate to each area depends on where we are in life. For example, our early years are primarily devoted to learning, our young-adult and middle years to earning and our later years to living and giving. Obviously we want to be engaged in all four activities throughout our lives, but the allocation will depend on where we are and what we want. Actively investing time means deciding what you want, making conscious choices to live that life and spending your time accordingly.

Money, on the other hand, should be invested passively. Passive investing means buying and holding no-load, low-cost index mutual funds with performances reflecting that of entire markets. Here's the plan in a nutshell:

1. Choose how you want to allocate your investment money among stocks, bonds and cash. You might allocate your investments this way:

- 50% domestic stocks
- 20% international stocks
- 20% bonds
- 10% cash

This decision is called "asset allocation," and it will have the greatest impact on your future returns.

2. Buy no-load, low-cost index funds according to that allocation. Put 50% in a total U.S. stock-market index fund, 20% in a total international-stock index fund, 20% in a total bond-market index fund and 10% in a money-market fund.

3. Contribute at least 10% of every dollar you earn to the portfolio. The more you contribute, the sooner you reach financial freedom.

4. Check the portfolio once a year. If your allocation of stocks is within 10% of the original allocation, do nothing.

Rebalance it whenever your stock allocation varies more than 10% from your plan.

That's all there is to it. It's no-brainer investing that outperforms at least 70% of the investment gurus who get paid to manage money. Best of all, implementing it takes little time and minimal financial knowledge. It's a financial plan that anyone who can understand and calculate simple percentages can do.

WHY IS IT A SECRET?

Why do I call LeBoeuf's Law the best-kept investment secret in the world? It must be a secret, because the overwhelming majority of people do the exact opposite: They invest time passively and money actively.

That great philosopher Yogi Berra said, "You can observe a lot just by watching." You don't have to be an observer for very long to realize that most people manage their time like sheep. Instead of taking charge, they let circumstances and others dictate how their days are spent. They allow others to tell them when to get up, when to go to work, what activities to perform, when to go home and how much they get paid for their time. Then one day they wake up and realize that they're spending their lives in the time/money trap.

When it comes to investing money, most people do one of two things. Approximately two thirds of them pay brokers, financial planners and/or money managers hefty sums to actively manage their money. Those fees and commissions contribute to the investment pro's wealth instead of the investor's. The sad truth is that most investment professionals charge their clients fees and commissions for underperforming the market most of the time. The vast majority of brokers, money managers, mutual-fund managers and financial planners get paid to deliver smaller returns than clients could make on their own by investing in index funds. Most don't add value. They reduce value and charge clients for it. (Is that why some are called "brokers"?)

Other investors choose to go it alone and manage their own money. The typical do-it-yourself investor wastes countless hours of time trying to beat the market. He spends enormous amounts of time and energy agonizing over what investments to buy, when to buy and when to sell.

Frank's Story

Frank (not his real name) is a thirty-year-old husband and father who got swept up in the tech-investing mania of the late nineties. He posted his story on an Internet discussion board for all to see and learn from:

It all started four years ago, when my best friend asked me if I'm investing money for retirement and for my family's future. I replied that all the money I have is in my bank account. So he told me about the stock market, mutual funds, how millions of people are investing for retirement, their children's education, and the potential risk and rewards. He also told me that the best way to invest is in the total market through index funds.

Before investing my money I decided to read and learn more about investing. I started watching investment news programs, read newspaper and magazine articles about the stock market and did a lot of research on the Web. It was 1997 and the market was booming. Companies like Dell, Cisco and Intel were doubling every year. Others, like Amazon and Yahoo, were tripling every year. I was very excited and confused. Why should I invest in index funds aver-

aging 17 to 20% a year, at that time, when I can buy a few good stocks and triple my money within a year? And that's what I did.

I was lucky and in four months I doubled my money. I wasn't a day trader and held stocks for an average of three months. In the beginning of 1998 I did my taxes and realized that a 95% gain was actually a 58% gain after taxes. It wasn't 95%, but 58% was still a great return on my investment. I asked my friend why he invested in boring index funds (by that time I thought I knew all about indexes and the mutual-fund industry) when he could double his money by investing in stocks much quicker. His response was: "Invest simply! Past performance is no guarantee of future results." When I asked him what he thought about a few companies, he said that he had never heard of them.

I was shocked. "How can you invest in the market and not know about the hottest stocks out there?" I asked.

He said, "That's what indexes are for. You simply invest in the total market. Have an asset-allocation plan and stick with it!" I thought it was stupid at the time.

I finished 1998 with 16% gain after taxes. When technology was on the rise in 1999 I invested in technology mutual funds so I could own more stocks. I did very well in 1999 and my average gain was 105%. Wow! After I did my taxes the net gain for 1999 was only 48%.

And then came the year 2000. I picked the best technology companies and funds for the past year and invested all my money in them. Before 2000 I had never lost any money in the market, so I was planning to double or maybe even triple my money.

You probably know what happened with technology in 2000. I lost 76% that year and more the following year. It was the most *difficult year of my life. I was watching my money melt like snow. First I thought it was just a brief correction and believed the NASDAQ would come back soon. I didn't want to sell and miss the rally. So I stayed with the market and ended up losing everything I had gained, plus a big chunk of my own money. As for my friend, he lost 4% of his portfolio in 2000 and was very happy to be in Vanguard index funds.*

After learning more about indexing, I transferred my investments to index funds.

What did I gain in those four years? Nothing. What did I lose? I lost a lot of time, a lot of money and a lot of confidence. I had severe anxieties and was overstressed almost all the time. For four years I spent ten hours a day on the Internet researching and reading about companies. I spent a tremendous amount of time reading investment magazines and newspapers. My car radio was always tuned to business stations. I was always too busy for my son and my wife.

I regret how I spent those four years very much. Don't be like me. Don't spend all your time looking for the best stock or fund, because you'll never find it. Don't chase after big returns or try to beat the market, because the odds are that the market will beat you. Life is short and IT IS NOT WORTH IT! There's more to life than the stock market. Simplify. Invest smart, invest safe, invest for life. Enjoy your friends, enjoy your family and don't forget to smell the roses.

The research is clear and conclusive: Trading is hazardous to your wealth, and market timing doesn't work for the vast majority. Passive investing over the long term is the least time-consuming and lowest-cost investment method; it is highly tax-efficient and very effective. The important thing is to have a plan and to start investing now. Waiting for the ideal time or believing that some investment expert is going to come into your life with a sure-fire formula to beat the market is pure fantasy. As the Prussian military theorist Karl von Clausewitz wrote, "The greatest enemy of a good plan is the dream of the perfect plan." He who waits for the perfect plan waits forever.

Invest your time actively and your money passively. It's the best-kept investment secret in the world. It's so simple, so obvious and so rarely practiced. If more people did use it, there would be more people with fortunes living the life of their dreams and fewer people with frowns. Don't waste your time playing the market. Own the market, live your life and enjoy the journey. That's the essence of LeBoeuf's Law.

THE MASTER KEY TO WEALTH

Simplicity gives us the power to do less of what doesn't matter—and gives us the power to do more of what does matter.

—JOHN C. BOGLE, FOUNDER
AND CHAIRMAN EMERITUS,
THE VANGUARD GROUP

The master key to wealth can be summed up in just one word: *simplicity*. Does that surprise you? Do you disagree?

I can assure you, there was a time when I would have vehemently disagreed, too. I worked in a university environment, where things are supposed to be complicated. I used to think, "How can getting and staying rich be simple?" Have you ever tried to decipher what Alan Greenspan is saying? Have you ever tried to read business textbooks filled with complex equations and financial theories? Have your eyes ever glazed over while you listened to economists and Wall Street gurus speaking in tongues as they foretold the future or tried to convince you why you should or shouldn't have your money in the stock market?

While the stock market, the economy or even your own

income-tax return may be complicated, that's precisely why you need to learn the simple keys to building wealth. The paradox of our time is that as things become increasingly complex, the more we need simplicity. We must practice a few simple rules that work and not allow ourselves to become sidetracked by the complexity of daily living.

You may be thinking, "Wait a minute, Michael. Don't get simplistic on me. A little knowledge is a dangerous thing." That can be true, and I would encourage you to read and learn as much as you want about wealth building, time management and financial planning. As a former professor, I'm all for education.

However, it's also true that a little knowledge can be a wonderful thing—if it's the right knowledge. Some cases in point:

- $E=MC^2$
- Do unto others as you would have them do unto you.
- Buy low, sell high.
- Smoking can kill you.
- Price is determined by supply and demand.
- Buckle up.

While enormous amounts of research and experience led to these conclusions, their simplicity is what makes them useful and easy to apply. The simplest ideas are the most powerful.

There are two simple but extremely powerful rules for managing time and building wealth. The key to managing time is the 80/20 Rule. The key to accumulating wealth is the Rule of 72. Both have been around for years, and if you are familiar with them, please feel free to go to Insight 4.

THE 80/20 RULE

In the nineteenth century, economist and sociologist Vilfredo Pareto discovered that 80% of the land in Italy was owned by

20% of the population. Then he noticed that 20% of the pea pods
in his garden yielded 80% of the peas harvested. After identify-
ing a few more examples that seemed to fit this pattern, he the-
orized what has become known as the Pareto Principle, or the
80/20 Rule: *Given a large number of items, a high percentage
of the value of the items (80%) is concentrated in relatively few of
the items (20%)*. While the ratio of 20% of the items yielding 80%
of the value isn't exact, it seems to be a good rule of thumb. Here
are just a few examples that appear to validate the 80/20 Rule:

- 80% of the dollar volume of an inventory is concentrated
  in 20% of the items.
- 80% of your telephone calls will come from 20% of the
  people who call you.
- 80% of the meals ordered in a restaurant come from 20%
  of the items on the menu.
- 80% of your headaches are caused by 20% of your problems.
- 80% of sales come from 20% of the customers.
- 80% of product complaints come from 20% of the products.
- 80% of an advertising campaign will produce 20% of the
  results.
- 80% of all television viewing is done during 20% of the
  time.
- 80% of your interruptions come from 20% of the people
  who interrupt you.

While it has many applications, the 80/20 Rule lies at the
heart of good time management. Simply put, 80% of your effec-
tiveness comes from doing 20% or less of what you have to do.

Here's a true story that illustrates the point. When Charles
Schwab (not the founder of today's Charles Schwab Corp.)
became president of Bethlehem Steel, he made consultant Ivy Lee

the following offer: "Show my staff and me a way to get more things done in less time and I'll pay you any fee within reason."

"Fine," said Lee. "I can give you something in twenty minutes that will step up your output at least fifty percent."

"Okay," Schwab replied. "I have just about that much time before I have to catch a train. What's your idea?"

Lee took a three-by-five card out of his pocket, handed it to Schwab and said, "Write down the six most important things you have to do tomorrow and number them in order of their importance. Now put this paper in your pocket, and first thing tomorrow morning, look at item one and start working on it until you finish it. Then do item two and so on. Do this until quitting time and don't be concerned if you have finished only one or two. You'll be working on the most important ones first, anyway. If you can't finish them all by this method, you couldn't have by any other method, and without some system, you probably wouldn't have even decided which was most important."

Lee waited while Schwab wrote his list. Then he said, "Try this system every working day. After you've convinced yourself of its value, have your employees try it. Try it as long as you wish and then send me a check for what you think it's worth."

Two weeks later Schwab sent Lee a $25,000 check for that twenty-five-minute consultation. He said Lee's advice was the most profitable he had ever taken. He later credited that lesson with turning the unknown Bethlehem Steel into the biggest independent steel producer in the world in less than five years, and earning him a $100 million fortune in the process. That was an enormous sum of money in the early twentieth century.

Was Schwab foolish to pay so much for such a simple idea? He didn't think so. "Sure it was a simple idea," Schwab said. "But what ideas are not basically simple? For the first time, my entire team and myself are getting first things done first."

First things first. That's the key to good time management

in three simple words. And that's why the 80/20 Rule is the master key to managing time. Success comes from investing your time in a few high-value activities with big payoffs and ignoring the many trivial ones.

Put the 80/20 Rule to work in your life. Make a daily to-do list at the start of each day as Charles Schwab did. Then rank your items in order of importance, either numbering them, as Schwab did, or using the A, B, C method. The items are first put in three categories: A) must do, B) should do and C) nice to do.

Then each set of goals is ranked in order. Your top-priority item is labeled A-1. Start with A's; and do C's only if you complete all the A's and B's.

Choice One covers how to set lifetime and intermediate goals. Like daily goals, they need to be ranked in order of importance. Whether the goals are lifetime, intermediate or daily, get in the habit of ranking them in order of importance and spend the bulk of your time achieving the few that have the highest payoffs. Doing this gets you a great return on your most important asset—your time.

THE RULE OF 72

The power of compound interest never ceases to amaze me. I'm not alone, because Albert Einstein considered it humankind's most powerful invention. While the 80/20 Rule says that we get more done by focusing our efforts on doing a few things well, the Rule of 72 shows us how time and the power of compound interest can effortlessly turn a few dollars into financial freedom.

Like the 80/20 Rule, the Rule of 72 is sheer simplicity. To determine approximately how many years it will take an investment to double in value, just divide 72 by the annual rate of return. For example, an investment that returns 9% per year doubles every 8 years ($72 \div 9 = 8$). Similarly, an investment that returns 12% doubles every 6 years (72 ÷ 12 = 6), and an investment that returns 18% doubles every 4 years (72 ÷ 18 = 4).

Once you know the Rule of 72, you begin to understand how a small investment becomes serious money over time. A single, onetime investment of $5,000 in a stock fund that earns 12% annually grows to $85,000 in 25 years and to $263,998 in 35 years.

If you want proof that the power of compound interest can make anyone a multimillionaire, consider this: If you saved a dollar a day, or $365 a year, from the day you were born, you would be worth over $2 million on your sixty-fifth birthday with a 10% rate of return. Get an 11% return, which is a little less than the stock market has returned over the long haul, and you'd be worth $4.2 million. A 12% return earns you $7.4 million. If you were afraid of stocks, invested in bonds and got a 7% return, you would still have $488,000. Did anybody teach you that in school? They sure didn't teach it to me.

Of course, that example makes some pretty heavy assumptions. You have to start saving from the day you were born, or have someone doing it for you. You can't touch the money for sixty-five years, you have to keep it all away from the tax collector and you have to realize that inflation will diminish the purchasing power of your nest egg. The Rule of 72 cuts both ways. A 4% annual rate of inflation halves the purchasing power of money every eighteen years. Nevertheless, it does illustrate how anyone investing less than most of us spend on coffee, soda pop or snack foods each day can become richer than he or she ever would have imagined.

Here's another interesting illustration that you can use to teach your children about the power of compounding money over time. Pose this question: If someone offered you a choice of $1 million today or a penny that would double every day for thirty days, which would you take? Most people would find it hard to turn down $1 million, but the lump sum is the wrong choice. A penny doubled every day for thirty days compounds to over $5 million, as illustrated in the following table.

DOUBLING A PENNY A DAY FOR THIRTY DAYS

DAY	AMOUNT	DAY	AMOUNT
1	1¢	16	$327.68
2	2¢	17	$655.36
3	4¢	18	$1310.72
4	8¢	19	$2621.44
5	16¢	20	$5242.88
6	32¢	21	$10485.76
7	64¢	22	$20,971.52
8	$1.28	23	$41,934.04
9	$2.56	24	$83,886.08
10	$5.12	25	$167,772.16
11	$10.24	26	$335,544.32
12	$20.48	27	$671,088.64
13	$40.96	28	$1,342,177.28
14	$81.92	29	$2,684,354.56
15	$163.84	30	$5,368,709.12

If you had the ability to double your money once a month and started with only one penny, that penny would grow to:

- $40.96 at the end of one year
- $167,772.16 at the end of two years
- $687,194,767.38 at the end of three years

Want a practical application that can make a young couple wealthy? If a couple contributes $3,000 each to a Roth IRA annually for forty years, their total investment is $240,000. Assuming a 10% rate of return, their Roth IRA will be worth $2,655,555 at the end of forty years—tax-free!

If You Think Education Is Expensive, Try Ignorance

While the Rule of 72 is a simple, powerful, wealth-building tool, it remains virtually unknown to the majority of Americans. Consider the findings reported from a 1999 survey sponsored by the Consumer Federation of America and the financial-services firm Primerica:

- One quarter of Americans believe their best chance to build wealth for retirement is to play the lottery. Twenty-eight percent believe that winning the lottery is their best chance to obtain $500,000 or more in their lifetime. In truth, the odds of winning a big lottery jackpot are between ten and twenty million to one.
- Only 47% said that saving and investing some of their income was the most reliable road to wealth.
- People were asked how much $25 invested weekly for 40 years at a 7% annual yield would amount to. Less than a third guessed over $150,000. The correct answer is $286,640.
- When asked how much $50 invested weekly at 9% for 40 years would yield, 37% had no idea and only 33% thought it would be over $300,000. The correct answer: $1,026,853.

If you're a young person, you might think, "That sounds great, Michael. But I don't want to wait until I'm old and decrepit to get rich." Or perhaps you're middle-aged and thinking, "Thanks a lot, Michael. Where were you when I was twenty?" To both I say, "Relax and keep reading." While compound interest is the master key to accumulating wealth, it isn't the only one, and we will be covering more in the pages ahead.

Never pass up the opportunity to benefit from the Rule of 72 and the power of compound interest. It's an effortless money-maker that every current and future millionaire makes good use of. If you ever wondered how the rich get richer, now you know.

THE TWENTIETH CENTURY'S
GREATEST GIFT

The fools who sing all summer weep all winter.

—JEWISH SAYING

In 1900 the life expectancy in the U.S. was forty-five for men and forty-seven for women. Thanks to advances in medical science and higher living standards, it's over thirty years higher today.

Consider what this means. We have doubled our number of adult years. We have been given the gift of a second middle age. Most important, our senior years will be much healthier and more enjoyable than those of our parents and grandparents. And with the human genome project in its infancy, there is no telling how many years and how much vigor will be added to our lives in the coming decades. At the beginning of the twentieth century, life expectancy was increasing at the rate of one tenth of 1% per year. At the end of the twentieth century, life expectancy was increasing at the rate of 1% per year.

This wonderful longevity bonus comes with the challenge of having to provide financially for many more years of life. At first glance, this may seem like another financial burden when you're trying to get out of the time/money trap. However, it's great news if you rethink your approach to money and apply the Rule of 72. Thirty more years means more time for your investments to compound and make you very, very rich. So what do you do? I recommend the following three things:

1. *Resolve to Make the Most of Your Longevity Bonus.* Consider this: *If you are over twenty years of age, most of your future will probably be spent on the north side of fifty.* The fastest-growing segment of today's population is people over eighty-five. According to a study by Mouton & Company, among couples who reach sixty-five there is a 16% chance that one will live to be a hundred, and some experts believe this percentage could double in the near future. Live as though you'll celebrate the big 1-0-0 someday, and don't be surprised if you do.

Take good care of yourself and treat your body like you're going to need it for a long, long time. Aging and illness are not the same things. Getting older is wonderful as long as you're healthy. As one who has lived six decades, I can tell you that each new decade has been better than the last. I'm not sure I could have said that had I been in poor health. Make it your goal to die young at the oldest possible age.

2. *Create Your Own Endowment.* You may be familiar with the concept of endowed chairs at colleges and universities. A philanthropist or a corporation donates a large sum of money to a university to create an endowed chair. The money is then invested and the proceeds used to fund a professor's salary and research expenses for an indefinite period of time. These positions are real academic plums, and the money and perks usually attract top-name scholars to fill them. If the professor leaves, retires or dies, the chair remains, and another premier scholar is hired to fill it.

Early in my university career, I realized that I had about a snowball's chance in hell of ever landing in an endowed chair. I enjoyed teaching and interacting with friends on the faculty but found the rest of the job meaningless and mundane. Writing scholarly research articles, presenting papers at professional meetings and serving on university committees had all the appeal of a root canal to me. I'm just not one who enjoys jumping through academic hoops, and you have to be an excellent hoop jumper to merit an endowed chair.

But one day, when I was about thirty-five, I had an epiphany that changed everything. A little voice inside of me said, "Why don't you endow your own chair?" Eureka!

From then on I went to work to create my own endowment. I started writing books, speaking and doing management consulting alongside my university job. I lived on my professor's salary, and most of what I earned moonlighting was used to fund my own private chair. Endowed chairs usually have lofty, impressive-sounding names, so I jokingly named my chair "The Homestead Chair of Academic Freedom": I lived on Homestead Avenue, and once the chair was sufficiently funded, I would achieve true academic freedom—freedom from academia. I could retire and do whatever I wanted for the rest of my life. Better yet, unlike a university chair, the Homestead Chair requires no work. It's a recliner.

The lesson is obvious: Endow thyself. Think like a capitalist instead of an employee. Don't earn just to spend. Resolve to build a nest egg of at least $1 million, or twenty times the amount of money you currently spend or want to spend in a year. If you plan to work part-time or have other sources of income, subtract that yearly income from your yearly spending figure and multiply the new amount by twenty.

While there are all sorts of complicated formulas and work sheets for figuring precisely how much you'll need to be financially independent, twenty times your yearly spending is a good ballpark figure to shoot for. Once again, the goal is to create a simple plan and get on the road to the winner's circle. Don't wait for the perfect plan.

You may be thinking, "Why on earth do I need twenty times my annual withdrawals?" Based on decades of stock-market history, financial planners generally agree that you can expect a long-term rate of return of 5% after taxes and inflation. You have to stay ahead or even with taxes and inflation, or you risk eating away at the principal of your nest egg and running out of money before you run out of time. With twenty times your yearly expenses in investments, you can quit work at any age with little chance of going broke—assuming a 5% yearly rate of withdrawal. Of course, as your life expectancy decreases, you can withdraw more than 5%, and you should. But I'm assuming you don't want to wait until you're seventy to retire. Keep in mind that a sixty-five-year-old retiring today may easily live well beyond age ninety. Better to err on the side of caution. You don't want to outlive your money.

If the idea of accumulating twenty times your annual spending sounds impossible, I can assure you it isn't. It isn't easy, but plenty of us have done it. Developing the right skills, keeping your eyes open for opportunities and using your time well can skyrocket your earning power to levels that will astound you. And if you save and invest most of that extra money, you'll have the Rule of 72 multiplying it for you with no additional effort on your part. Your money will be making money while you sleep.

3. *Realize That Delayed Gratification Is Not Denied Gratification.* Remember that offer for the lifetime job in which you get a huge bonus for finishing early? It's not a pipe dream. It's an achievable reality, and I urge you to accept it. Most people don't even know the offer is on the table. Blinded by short-term thinking and a paycheck mentality, they earn to spend and stay in the time/money trap, oblivious to what their lives could be.

To be sure, getting out of the trap and into the winner's circle isn't easy. However, it can be done, and once you get there, you'll realize that the benefits are worth infinitely more than their price. You pay for every success in life with commitment and delayed gratification. There is no success of any kind without sacrifice. The key to exceptional success in any major endeavor requires investing some of your time, effort and money today for a much greater payoff tomorrow.

I'm not suggesting that you lead a life of great deprivation just so you can become a millionaire. I sure didn't, and I would consider it foolish to do so. Life is to be enjoyed, and today is all that's guaranteed. But please take a moment and imagine the wonderful life of financial freedom waiting for you if you think long-term and invest some of today's efforts and earnings toward building a much better tomorrow.

Make smart choices today, and you'll get to spend and enjoy the money when there's much, much more of it. And there's an added bonus: Knowing that you're building a better tomorrow makes you happier today.

Now that you see how great your future can be, let's look at the kinds of decisions that can turn that dream into a reality.

Part II

DO IT!

TEN CHOICES FOR ACHIEVING PERSONAL
AND FINANCIAL FREEDOM

We've got two lives—one we're given and the other one we make.

—*GOOD STUFF* MAGAZINE

YOU AND I HAVE PROBABLY NEVER MET, BUT I KNOW THIS MUCH ABOUT YOU: The millions of choices you made yesterday are the reason you are where you are today. All of us are the sum of our choices. The decisions we make determine what we do, and what we do determines our fate. It was true yesterday, it's true today and it will be true tomorrow.

Your tremendous power of personal choice is all you need to get from wherever you are to the winner's circle. People who buy lottery tickets and engage in other forms of gambling, hoping to get rich, have it all wrong. They're searching, wishing and hoping for some force outside themselves to step in and make them rich. But every self-made millionaire will tell you that wealth is the product of choice, not chance. It isn't the hand of cards you're dealt. It's how you play the hand.

The principles of wealth creation are 100% impartial. They aren't living beings, they have no feelings and they couldn't care less who gets rich and who doesn't. But the great thing about wealth principles is that anyone can use them. Self-made millionaires are people just like you. If you apply the principles and make the same smart choices that made them millionaires, you can achieve the same kind of wealth.

Based on LeBoeuf's Law for managing money and time, Part II teaches ten strategic choices that will get you to the winner's circle while avoiding ten common choices that would lead you into the time/money trap and keep you there.

LIVE THE LIFE YOU WANT INSTEAD OF THE LIFE OTHERS EXPECT

There is a sacred calling on your life, and the question is: Will you spend your life flittering and fluttering about, or take the time and really heed that call and create your own path to your highest good? . . . You cannot let other people define your life for you. You are the author of your own life. . . .

—Oprah Winfrey

Several friends e-mailed me the following story from an anonymous source:

An American businessman was at the pier of a small coastal Mexican village when a small boat with just one fisherman docked. Inside the small boat were several large yellowfin tuna. The American complimented the Mexican on the quality of his fish and asked how long it took to catch them.

The Mexican replied, "Only a little while."

The American then asked why he didn't stay out longer and catch more fish.

The Mexican said he had enough to support his family's immediate needs. The American asked, "But what do you do with the rest of your day?"

The fisherman replied, "I sleep late, fish a little, play with my children, take a siesta with my wife, Maria, stroll into the village each evening, where I sip wine and play the guitar with my *amigos*. I have a full and busy life, Señor."

The American scoffed, "I am a Harvard M.B.A. and could help you. You should spend more time fishing and, with the proceeds, buy a bigger boat, and with the proceeds from the bigger boat, you could buy several boats. Eventually you would have a fleet of fishing boats. Instead of selling your catch to a middleman you would sell directly to the processor, eventually owning your own cannery. You would control the product, processing and distribution. You would need to leave this small coastal fishing village and move to Mexico City, then Los Angeles and eventually New York, where you would run your expanding enterprise."

The Mexican fisherman asked, "But Señor, how long will all of this take?"

The American replied, "Probably fifteen to twenty years."

"But what then, Señor?"

The American laughed and said, "That's the best part. When the time was right, you would announce an IPO and sell your company stock to the public and become very rich. You would make millions!"

"Millions, Señor? Then what?"

The American said, "Then you would retire. Move to a small fishing village where you would sleep late, fish a little, play with your kids, take a siesta with your wife, stroll to the village in the evenings, where you could sip wine and play your guitar with your *amigos.*"

Perhaps someone e-mailed that story to you, too, because it has been widely circulated on the Internet. Its ubiquity tells me that there are a lot of us questioning our work and our life.

Are you dancing to the beat of your own music or to some-one else's? If it's the latter, *wake up!* You are financially and emotionally shortchanging yourself. The first and most important smart choice is to live the life you want when there are a myriad of other forces persuading you to do otherwise. The most successful people are the ones who decide what they want out of life—that's Priority One. Then they choose the kind of work, spouse, family structure, location and other major life components that are compatible with the lifestyle they want to live.

Unfortunately, most of us don't do that. Instead, we conform to the expectations of others in the hope of being accepted, admired, loved and respected. The problem is, the people we usually take our cues from are in the time/money trap, too. If you want to stay in the trap, just keep listening to and following them.

Please don't misunderstand me. I don't advocate that you become a radical counterconformist who does the exact opposite of what others do. That's worse than following the crowd. What I do advocate is getting in touch with the voice inside that tells you why you're here, what brings joy to your life and what you can do to enrich the world and yourself.

BEGIN WITH TWO QUESTIONS AND A DREAM

Have you ever taken the time to think about and decide what you really want out of life? Most of us are so busy *doing* that we don't take the time to answer life's big questions. That's too bad, because those are the questions that, when correctly answered, guarantee a successful and fulfilling life.

Here's what I want you to do: Choose a time and place where you can isolate yourself from the rest of the world for several hours or, better yet, several days. Think of it as a personal retreat. Friends, spouses and children aren't allowed. This is all about you getting in touch with you.

The environment should be one where you can relax and be isolated from the rest of the world. Maybe it's a cabin in the mountains or by the seashore. If that's not possible, driving to an isolated spot or checking in to a hotel will do. Just get away from it all. No distractions allowed. Bring a pen and a writing pad or, if you prefer, a laptop computer.

Once you're situated and relaxed, you want to find the answers to these two questions:

1. What do I want out of life?
2. How will I know when I have it?

More specifically, picture the kind of life you would love to live, doing the things you want to do when you want to do them, and write the answers to these questions:

- Where would you live?
- What would you do with your life if you had all the money you needed and the time to enjoy it?
- Who would be with you?
- How would you use your God-given talents?
- What activities do you find so engrossing that they cause you to lose all track of time?
- What activities bring you the most joy and personal satisfaction?
- What's the one thing you would love to do if you knew you couldn't fail?
- How does it feel knowing that your time and your life are your own?

Don't censor your thoughts. Write rapidly, putting down whatever comes into your mind. There are no right or wrong answers.

Repeat this exercise several times over a period of days or

weeks. Once you feel you have thoroughly explored what you want from life, combine all your answers into one consolidated document that describes the life of your dreams on one page. This is your personal vision statement.

Just as Michelangelo saw the *David* before he created it, you have to visualize the life of your dreams before you can live it. Once you have a clear picture of the kind of life you want to live, you can begin to set meaningful goals and work toward making that dream come true. But you have to dream first, because dreams inspire and make all the planning and work worthwhile. Martin Luther King, Jr., didn't motivate a nation to undergo enormous change by saying, "I have a goal." He said, "I have a dream!"

Nick Carter Trades a Job for a Dream Come True

My friend Arnold "Nick" Carter is a vice president of Nightingale-Conant Corporation, where he has enjoyed a stellar career for over thirty years. He worked closely with the late Earl Nightingale, one of the twentieth century's greatest minds on the topic of success and human potential. Earl's radio show, *Our Changing World,* aired five days a week on over a thousand stations to an audience of forty million listeners. In addition, Earl, with his business partner, Lloyd Conant, founded the audio-cassette industry with the Nightingale-Conant Corporation. Here is Nick's fascinating story, in his own words, of how he turned an imaginary conversation with Earl Nightingale into a thirty-year love affair with his work:

I met Earl first on the road, listening to his radio show, Our Changing World, *which to me was the greatest show I ever heard. And I was on my way to Martin Marietta to work, where I was head of customer relations. And he said, "Hello, Nick," to me on the radio.*

And I said, "Hello, Earl."

He said, "What are you doing?"

I said, "I'm on my way to work at Martin Marietta. We make missiles for defense against enemies."

"Oh, I see. And, uh, is this the job you want to do with your life?"

"Well, no, but I have a wife and two kids, and I've got to provide a living for them."

"Now wait a minute," he said, "I want to make sure I have this straight. In the one chance you have at life, you're telling me you're in a job you don't really want to be in?"

And I said, "Well, in a way, yes."

He said, "Are you nuts? Are you crazy? Now, whatever you have to do, you only have one shot on the earth, buddy-boy, so if you have to dynamite yourself out, get out of that job into what you'd like to do! What would you like to do?"

"Well, I'd like to work for you, Earl."

"What do you mean?"

"Well, you're a guy who brings great truth to people, lifts them and makes their lives happier and more successful."

"I see. Okay."

And I got into my office and I couldn't even think. I was just numb. I said, "I've got to get out of here. Some way." Now, I think the Lord enters into things sometimes, and two weeks later I was meeting Earl Nightingale in a receiving line at the Gold Key Inn in Orlando, Florida, in January 1970. And next to him was his partner, Lloyd Conant.

And I said, "Mr. Nightingale, I just love your work. You've helped me so much with your ideas and the way you get right into the core of things. And I just want to thank you, sir. And if you're ever interested, sir, I think I have a way to double your sales."

Now that was exactly the right thing to say to Earl Nightingale. And instead of saying, "Get away from me, boy, you bother me," he said, "How would you do that?"

I gave him a little one-minute summary. He took out his card and put his home address on Lakeshore Drive in Chicago on it. He said, "Send me that handwritten one-page so I can look at it. I want to think about it."

Well, a few weeks later I had a call from his partner, Lloyd Conant, and he said, "Earl tells me you have a way to double our sales. We'd like you to come to Chicago tonight."

"Well, I can't. I'm speaking tomorrow at Cape Kennedy, sir."

"Well, come up Monday, then."

"I have meetings all over the place here at Martin Marietta, sir."

"When can you come up?"

"How about next Friday?"

"Next Friday it is. Land, go to the hotel there in Lincolnwood and we'll see you for dinner."

They gave me three hours at a blackboard to show them how I'd double their sales. And at the end of that, Earl said, "Would you like to work here?"

And I said, "Well, Mr. Nightingale, I, I, I have thought about that, that I'd like to work with Socrates if I could, you know."

And he said to me, "When would you like to start and how much do you want to start?"

Now at that very moment—I don't know whether you can read into this what I'm trying to tell you, ladies and gentlemen—but at that very moment my life changed for the better. Why? Because in the one shot I had at life, I was going to be in a company that was doing exactly what I wanted to do, which was bring truth to people to lift them.

There are too many people in the world who are living by wrong ideas or wrong concepts. And Nightingale was trying to get them to see how to be happy and successful and to bring out the best they had. So that was a very, very lucky series of events. And that's why I say, sometimes I think the Higher Power comes in to help you get where you want to be. And so, Higher Power, if you're listening up there, I just want you to know I really appreciate the chance to be here for the last thirty years doing what I love to do.

In case you're wondering, Nick Carter is a millionaire, too. He helped build a business he loves and shared in the prosperity.

TRANSLATE YOUR DREAMS INTO GOALS

Envisioning the life of your dreams is vital. Albert Einstein said, "Imagination is more important than knowledge." Yet for all the inspiration and motivation they inspire, dreams alone won't get you anywhere near the winner's circle. It's just a beginning. Creating the millionaire in you requires roots and wings. Dreams are wings. Goals and the action needed to achieve them are roots. Dreams without goals and action are meaningless fantasies. Goals and action without dreams are drudgery. You need all three. Here's a good formula to keep in mind: dreams + goals + action = success.

Over a century ago, Henry Ford had a dream of every American family owning their own car. It seemed impossible at the time because cars were handmade, one at a time, by craftsmen and were much too expensive for the average American family. We all know that Ford achieved his dream in spades because most American families own two or more cars today. How did he do it? He translated the dream into goals and the goals into action plans; then he broke the action plans into specific, small tasks with deadlines for completion. The process of building a car was broken down into an assembly line of minute tasks that anyone could perform efficiently with very little training. It reduced the cost of production to the point that almost every family could afford a Ford.

The process is the same for making any dream come true, including yours. You begin with a dream, set lifetime goals for realizing it, create a set of action plans and list activities that need to be completed to achieve the goals. It isn't hocus-pocus. It's focus-focus. Here are some guidelines to help you:

1. *Be sure your goals are yours and yours alone.* Only you know what's best for you. Don't set goals that other people think are important. It's a great idea to ask others for feedback or to bounce your ideas off of them. In fact, friends and relatives may see talents and passions in you that you don't. But the final decisions on your goals are yours and yours alone. *It's your life.*

2. *Use the BEST criteria for setting goals.* BEST is an acronym to remind you that goals should be:

- Believable: Don't sell yourself short. You can probably achieve more than you think you can. Aim high, but don't set impossible goals. You want battles big enough to matter but small enough to win.

- Energizing: Set goals that excite you and give you a reason to get up in the morning and tackle them.
- Specific: Clarify and quantify the definition of successful achievement at the outset.
- Timed: Every goal should have a deadline for achievement. If it doesn't have a deadline, it isn't a goal; it's a fantasy.

For example, "I want to be rich someday" isn't a BEST goal, it's just wishful thinking. A BEST goal is "I will have a portfolio worth $2 million fifteen years from today."

3. *Write down your goals and read them frequently.* Writing down your goals increases clarity and commitment. Would you build your dream home without blueprints? Well, your goals are the blueprints for the life of your dreams. Setting down what you need to achieve forces you to think clearly about what needs to be done. Reading and following your written goals dramatically increases the odds of achieving them.

4. *Set goals for every major area of your life.* Several years ago at a university commencement address, Brian Dawson of Coca-Cola Enterprises gave the graduates some excellent advice:

> *Imagine life as a game in which you are juggling some five balls in the air. You name them—work, family, health, friends and spirit. You will soon recognize that work is a rubber ball. If you drop it, it will bounce back. But the other four balls—family, health, friends and spirit—are made of glass. If you drop one of these, they will be irrevocably scuffed.*

Living a balanced life is important. Since you're reading this book, I assume that one of your goals is to become a millionaire and have the time to enjoy your money. That's an admirable and worthwhile goal. But what good is becoming a millionaire if it costs you your health or your family, or requires doing something that scars your conscience? Wealth is only a means to an end.

Take the time to set other lifetime goals in addition to becoming a millionaire. Here are some categories that you might consider:

- Career goals: What kind of career would really excite you? Don't fall into the trap of doing something just because it comes easily to you. It's important to have the talent *and* the passion for it. Thousands of years ago Aristotle wrote, "Where the needs of the world and your talents cross, there lies your vocation." If you enjoy your current career, what can you do to get better at it?
- Family goals: What can you do to improve your relationship with your spouse and children? If you're not married but would like to be, what can you do to improve those odds?
- Recreational goals: Everyone needs to get away from it all occasionally to recharge. What would you like to do?
- Health and wellness goals: What can you do to ensure and improve your health? The best medicine is preventive.
- Community goals: What can you volunteer or contribute to improve the area where you live?
- Personal relationship goals: What can you do to maintain and improve the friendships with people you care about? What can you do to meet more of the kind of people you would most enjoy?
- Self-esteem goals: What one or two things can you do that would bolster your self-confidence and make you feel great about yourself?

- Religious and spiritual goals: What can you do to strengthen the inner peace and faith you need to lead a fulfilling and purposeful life?

The best goals will improve your life in several areas. Going back to school to get an advanced degree might bolster your career, your income and your self-esteem. Working in an animal-rescue shelter to find homes for homeless animals can be a spiritual and community goal as well as a way to meet people who share your compassion and concern. Starting a lifelong diet and exercise program with your spouse or a friend can be an excellent health, relationship and self-esteem goal. The best type of goal improves your life in several areas; the more areas, the better.

5. *Check your goals for compatibility and set priorities.* Overlook this component and you set yourself up for frustration and fatigue. Too many of us try to do it all. Sorry, it's impossible. You can't be all things to all people. While it might be possible to be a wonderful homemaker, high-powered corporate executive, president of the Junior League, super wife and terrific soccer mom over the course of a lifetime, there aren't enough hours in the day for anyone to excel at all five at the same time. Rank your goals in order of importance and pursue those that work in harmony to help you achieve your dream. Life is the art of the possible.

6. *Translate your goals into action plans.* Action plans are intermediate goals that bridge the gap between a daily to-do list and lifetime achievements. They're usually projects that take less than a year but more than a day to complete. For example, my intermediate goal at this moment is to write this book. Well-thought-out action plans ensure that your daily activities contribute to the achievement of lifetime goals.

Setting lifetime goals doesn't mean they are carved in stone. Update them once a year. As time goes by, your list of lifetime

An Action-Planning Exercise

Here's an exercise to help you think through an intermediate-range goal you would like to achieve. Choose one of your most important lifetime goals. Take several sheets of paper and answer the following questions and statements:

1. State clearly and specifically a goal you would like to achieve in the next year.
2. Why do you want to achieve this goal?
3. If you succeed, what will it do for you?
4. What would you consider to be a moderate success? A good success? A tremendous success? Be specific.
5. How much do you want to achieve this goal?
6. How will achieving this goal contribute to the accomplishment of your lifetime goals?
7. What price will you have to pay to achieve this goal? Are you willing to pay it?
8. Estimate your chances of achieving this goal.
9. What will happen if you aren't successful? Can you live with it?
10. List the major subgoals involved in achieving this goal and assign a target date to each.
11. What obstacles stand between you and successful completion of this project?
12. What can you do today that will start you on the path to achieving this goal?

goals will change. New goals will be added and old ones dropped. That's fine and to be expected. Much of successful living and personal growth comes from learning through trial and error.

Finally, don't expect things to always go according to plan, because the one thing you can be sure of is they won't. An old Yiddish proverb says, "Man plans, God laughs." But those who have a clear picture of what they want and go after it are infinitely more likely to enjoy the life of their dreams than those who passively sit back and let life happen. Looking at my own life, I'm amazed at how wonderful opportunities magically appear when I know what I want and go after it. In truth, it isn't magic at all. It's opportunity meeting preparation.

STACK THE ODDS IN YOUR FAVOR
INSTEAD OF AGAINST YOU

Long-term gain is never the result of short-term thinking.

—Anonymous

A cartoon pictures two guys looking at a ladder labeled "The Ladder of Success." One guy solemnly says to the other, "I was hoping it would be an escalator."

The ladder to the winner's circle isn't an escalator, either—unless you happen to choose rich parents, marry a wealthy person, win the lottery or a casino jackpot. As Donald Kendall noted, "The only place success comes before work is in the dictionary." You have to be willing to climb the ladder.

What most of us don't realize is that through your power of choice you can, to a great degree, control the length of the ladder and the difficulty of the climb. Most of us unwittingly make the climb a lot tougher than it has to be. The way to take control has to do with a four-letter word that many of us don't understand or like to think about: RISK.

Does the thought of taking major risks make you uneasy? If it does, welcome to the club. Most of us don't like to take risks unless we have to. We like to feel comfortable and secure. Yet we all have to deal with risks and make major life choices. They're as much a part of life as eating and sleeping.

People tend to deal with risks in one of three ways, and two of them are likely to keep you in the time/money trap. The first way is to be a bold, fearless risk taker. It's common for motivational speakers to romanticize the need for bold risks. Perhaps you've read or heard some of the following all-too-common statements:

- Do what you fear and the fear will vanish.
- Feel the fear and do it anyway.
- Life is a daring adventure or nothing.—Helen Keller
- Live your dreams and let the chips fall where they may.
- Be bold, and mighty forces will come to your aid.
- We have nothing to fear but fear itself.—Franklin D. Roosevelt

Inspiring thoughts like that can really excite a crowd. So do science-fiction movies. But, like science-fiction movies, those statements ignore a large part of reality. People who fearlessly "go for it" can and do win big—sometimes. The problem is that by ignoring the downside that comes with every major risk, they lose more frequently than they win. Instead of steadily climbing the ladder of success, they ride the roller coaster of feast and famine.

You may know someone who has made a fortune, lost it all, made another fortune, lost it and so on. It's not rare (especially among motivational speakers), and it's certainly not boring. But it's not the shortest or surest way to reach the winner's circle and stay there. The dot-com millionaires are a case in point. Never before in history were so many so wealthy so briefly. Be bold, and mighty forces can leave you bankrupt, demoralized and homeless. That's the part motivational speakers rarely mention.

The second way people commonly deal with risk is to avoid it. These poor, timid souls let the potential downside of any risk blind them to the potential gains. Risk avoiders allow their fear of failure and the unknown to foreclose any chance of ever reaching the winner's circle. They stay in jobs or careers they don't like until age sixty-five because they feel secure and that's all they know. They stay in unhappy relationships or bad marriages because starting over is just too difficult and dangerous. They don't like where they live but wouldn't dream of moving to somewhere they might prefer because they don't know anybody there. And they wouldn't dream of investing in the stock market. It's too risky, and Grandpa lost everything in the Great Depression.

Through their own behavior, risk avoiders sentence themselves to mediocrity for life without parole. They may climb one or two rungs up the ladder but no higher because they insist on keeping one foot on the ground.

Contrary to popular belief, most people who reach the winner's circle and stay there aren't go-for-broke risk takers. In fact, most are rather cautious, including yours truly. Instead of being risk takers or risk avoiders, they opt for the third approach: to become good risk managers. When faced with a major risk, they gather as much information as they can, weigh the pluses and the minuses and decide if taking the chance is worth it. When the odds are in their favor, they go for it. If not, they ignore it and move on. Good risk managers don't win them all, but they win a lot more than they lose. The net result is a steady climb up the ladder to the winner's circle.

The Immigrant's "Edge"

Here's a fact that may surprise you: Legal immigrants to the United States become millionaires at four times the rate of natural-born citizens. The reason is simple—they see the U.S. as a nation of unlimited opportunity. They read and hear about the American Dream, come here with a vision and work very hard to make their dreams come true.

A few years ago I met a naturalized U.S. citizen from Iran. He owned several successful businesses and was a millionaire many times over. During the course of our conversation, he told me he wished that every American of eighteen years of age had to spend just one year earning a living in Iran with no help from home; after that year, he said young Americans would never again take their country for granted. It would open their eyes to incredible opportunities right in front of them and they would realize just how easy it is to make money in this country.

A graduate student from the Far East told me a similar story when I was teaching. He was in the U.S. on a two-year visa to get an M.B.A. He told me that he felt guilty spending those two years to get an education, because in his country, people believed that the privilege of spending two years in the U.S. was an invitation to get rich.

The next time you find yourself thinking that the odds of reaching the winner's circle are against you, keep this in mind: People immigrate to the U.S. every day and are confronted with the following obstacles:

- Learning a whole new language
- Assimilating an entirely new culture
- Earning the privileges of U.S. citizenship that the rest of us inherit
- Overcoming the prejudices of being an outsider

Despite those enormous hurdles, they still become million-aires at four times the rate of natural-born citizens.

Go to the mirror, look yourself straight in the eye and recite this little poem:

Roses are red,
Violets are blue.
If there's a millionaire in them,
There's a millionaire in you.

HOW TO STACK THE ODDS IN YOUR FAVOR

Being a smart risk taker is an essential part of reaching financial freedom. Most people don't become millionaires because they don't consider the odds of success and the financial implications of major life choices when they make them. Your journey to the winner's circle will likely be shorter and more pleasant to the degree that you follow the following seven guidelines.

1. *Get a good education but don't overpay.* Over 90% of today's millionaires are college graduates, and over half have advanced degrees. A person starting out with a bachelor's degree will earn about $17,000 per year more than a high school graduate. Master's-degree holders earn an additional $14,000, and professional-degree holders average $13,000 more than a master's. In addition to increased earning power, a good education increases your ability to live a richer, fuller life in ways that money can't buy.

Make sure you get the most for your education dollar, especially if you or your parents are footing the bill. Being admitted to a highly selective, private university is a wonderful opportunity if you can get a healthy financial-aid package. But if attending such a school means being saddled with a large postgraduate debt, it probably isn't worth it. Highly selective universities turn out highly successful graduates because they admit winners and then take the credit for their success. Most of their graduates have the talent and drive to succeed no matter where they go to school. Your local state university can provide you with an excellent education for a fraction of the cost. In today's world, knowledge travels at the speed of light. All schools use similar textbooks; the professors all read the same research in their respective fields; and we all surf the same Internet.

If your parents are willing to send you to an expensive, private university, calculate the difference between the cost of attending it and your local state university for four years. (The difference will probably be over $100,000.) Then tell them you want to go to State U. and ask them to invest the difference in no-load, low-cost index funds to finance either their retirement or yours. In addition to a good education, you'll get either two grateful parents or a shortcut to the winner's circle. With a little luck, you may get both.

2. *Choose the right kind of career.* The late entertainer George Burns gave the best career advice I ever heard: "Fall in love with what you do and you'll never work another day in your life." The right career for you isn't one that has the highest earning potential. Nor is it the one with the most prestige or the loftiest title. The right kind of career is one that:

- You enjoy and find meaningful
- Holds your interest
- Makes the most of your talents
- Gives you a feeling of accomplishment
- Enables you to live the lifestyle you want

You'll likely have several careers in your lifetime and may have to try a few until you get a good fit. I've had two careers. Being a professor led me to being a writer, speaker and consultant. My second career has been much more enjoyable and profitable than the first. Through trial and error, we live and learn.

The first major career choice you need to make is whether to be self-employed or to work for someone else. In today's free-agent economy, job security has gone the way of the steam locomotive, and an increasing number of us are opting to work as independent professionals. A survey by Aquent, a company that matches independent professionals with companies, reports that independent workers are happier with their work situations than those in traditional settings. The survey also found that independent professionals are two times more likely than employees to earn more than $75,000 per year.

Statistically speaking, the odds of reaching the winner's circle favor the self-employed business owner and professional. However, you can get there in fine style as an employee, too. There are plenty of millionaires who built their fortunes while employed as accountants, engineers, professors, salespersons, government employees and corporate executives. Don't make the mistake of believing that you have to be an entrepreneur to become a millionaire. It just isn't so.

Four words of caution if you're thinking about going into business for yourself: *don't buy a job!* Too many people borrow huge amounts of money, invest their life savings and work endless hours to build a business that returns less on their investment than they could have made investing in an index fund. Not only do they make an inferior return on their money, they waste enormous amounts of time that could have been invested in a paying job, spent with their families or doing whatever they want. Money is only money, but time is life. Know the business and get an objective third-party evaluation of the earnings potential before you commit yourself to it.

3. *Take steps to ensure good health.* This isn't a physical fitness book, so I'll be brief and to the point. If you smoke heavily, eat and drink excessively, live recklessly, expose yourself to a lot of stress and never exercise, you don't need a nest egg. The odds are you'll run out of time long before you reach the winner's circle and someone else will enjoy the fruits of your labor. Choose to be your own best friend and take care of yourself. Fiscal fitness without physical fitness is pointless.

4. *Live in an area with a low cost of living.* As you probably know, the cost of living varies enormously across the country. A willingness to relocate can greatly ease your climb to the winner's circle. It's much easier to save when you aren't burdened with enormous mortgage payments, high state and property taxes, huge home-heating costs and the like. In some states, you can pay over half of your annual earnings in federal, state and local taxes. Ouch!

Generally speaking, the most expensive places to live are on the Atlantic Coast between Washington and Boston, and on the Pacific Coast between San Diego and San Francisco. Lower costs of living and good earnings potential can be found in the Midwest, the South and the Southwest. One factor that really helped me grow my nest egg was living in the suburbs of New Orleans for a number of years in a house with no mortgage and no property taxes. Believe it or not, it was totally legal.

If you live in an expensive area and want to consider moving, check out the Salary Calculator online at homefair.com (http://www.homefair.com/calc/salcalc.html). You can compare your area's cost of living with other cities and towns you might enjoy living in. Try plugging a few cities in to the calculator and comparing them. It's a real eye-opener.

5. *Marry once to a frugal spouse who shares your vision of financial freedom.* Most people marry for romantic love, and I'm all for that. But it's also true that money disagreements are the number-one cause of matrimonial disharmony and divorce.

Money isn't a romantic subject, so most couples don't seriously discuss it until after they're married. Then the reality sets in that marriage is, among other things, a financial arrangement. This is not the time to find out that you love frugality and your spouse loves extravagant spending. A good marriage is built on shared values, with two people pulling in the same direction.

The financial implications of choosing the right spouse cannot be overstated. Two young people with incomes can make a goal of financial freedom come true in a relatively short time. On the other hand, a messy divorce can cost you half your wealth, plus legal fees, alimony or child support. After experiencing several divorces, the late humorist Lewis Grizzard wrote, "Instead of getting married again, I'm going to find a woman I don't like and give her a house."

If you're contemplating marriage, make sure you and your heart's desire are on the same page financially and share the same vision for the future. If you have substantial assets, give strong consideration to a prenuptial agreement. The unpleasant truth is that 50% of all marriages end in divorce. Almost every homeowner carries fire insurance, and nowhere near 50% of all homes burn down. Look objectively at the odds and do what's necessary to protect your assets before taking this most important calculated risk.

6. *Buy a moderately priced home.* I'm sure you've read or heard the arguments against homeownership that some of the New Age financial gurus expound: It's too expensive, there's too much upkeep, your money is tied up, you can't move as easily and investing in stocks will get you a better long-term return. That may be the logic, but the reality is that most Americans' net worth is in their homes. Take a look at these 1998 statistics from the Harvard University Center for Housing Studies, comparing homeowners with renters:

- Homeowners fifty-five and older had a median net worth of $177,400 and $80,000 in home equity; renters fifty-five and over had a median net worth of $5,500 with zero home equity.
- White homeowners had a median net worth of $148,920; white renters had a median net worth of $5,800.
- African-American homeowners had a median net worth of $67,280; African-American renters had a median net worth of $1,661.
- Hispanic homeowners had a median net worth of $70,000; Hispanic renters had a median net worth of $2,000.
- Asian and other homeowners had a median net worth of $163,800; Asian and other renters had a median net worth of $7,760.

If you want further evidence of the importance of home-ownership, *The New York Times* reported the following statistic on March 21, 1999: The average American homeowner retires with a net worth of $115,000. The average nonhomeowner retires with a net worth of only $800.

Virtually all millionaires are or have been homeowners. It's an asset that appreciates and forces you to save; it's a tax shelter and the foundation that most net worth is built on. Where people get into trouble with homeownership is buying more house than they can afford, or buying a house requiring expensive maintenance, then not staying in it long enough for significant appreciation. Don't spend more than 25% of your total income on your mortgage payment, insurance and taxes. For a good chance at a nice return on your investment, plan to stay in a house at least five years unless you decide to use the following wealth-building strategy:

The government gives those with handyman skills a great chance to build wealth tax-free. If you buy a house, live in it for two years and sell it, you get to keep up to $250,000 of the profits if you're single—or $500,000 if you're married—tax-free. Buy a fixer-upper, move in, work on improving it for two years, sell it for a handsome profit, invest some of the profits in an index fund, buy another fixer-upper and keep repeating the process. In time you'll be a millionaire.

If you're single and want to give homeownership a try, don't put it off waiting for Mr. or Ms. Right to come along. Why pay the landlord when you can pay yourself? My wife, Elke, and I both owned homes when we met. When we decided to get married, we used the money from the sale of both houses for the down payment on our dream home.

7. *Have a moderate number of children.* Not being a parent, I can't comment firsthand on all the rich and wonderful experiences that come with parenthood, although my friends tell me there are many. But I do know this: Children cost money—a whole lot of money. According to "Family Money Basics," published by the National Endowment for Financial Education and the American Humane Association, the estimated cost of rearing a child from birth to age seventeen is $117,000. Add on the college years and you're easily talking about a total cost of $175,000 to $200,000 per child.

I'm not trying to discourage you from having children. However, I would urge you to consider the financial cost and balance your desire for progeny with your goal of financial freedom. Most millionaires have two or three children. A good case can be made that the love of our children motivates us to work harder to provide the best for our families, resulting in more wealth. But at $175,000 per child, you'll need some serious motivation if you plan to have half a dozen children and reach the winner's circle, too.

In summary, the life choices you make with respect to education, career, health, location, marriage, homeownership and children will have an enormous impact on how quickly and easily you reach financial freedom. While I don't believe you should consider only the financial consequences of such decisions, it's foolhardy to ignore them. When I was a college freshman, I read a book that defined maturity as the ability to relate today's actions to tomorrow's results. Time and experience have convinced me that it's one of the best lessons I ever learned.

Twenty years later I was having coffee with a thirty-five-year-old university psychotherapist. I listened sympathetically as she complained about the low pay in her chosen profession. She said, "When I was twenty years old I thought, 'Money isn't important. All I need is enough for a little apartment, enough to feed and clothe myself, and I'll be happy.'" Then she paused, looked down at her coffee cup, looked back up and said, "You know what? That's bull****!"

BE A SUPER SAVER
INSTEAD OF A BIG SPENDER

Get what you can, and what you get, hold; 'tis the Stone that
will turn all your Lead into Gold.

—BENJAMIN FRANKLIN

Now we come to the choice that separates the serious future
millionaires from the wanna-bes. If you're a good saver, you'll
get there. If you're a poor saver, you won't. It's that simple.
Without saving, it makes no difference how hard you work,
how much you earn or how much you know about investing.
If you don't save, you don't have a prayer.

The overwhelming importance of saving was confirmed in
a study done by economists Steven Venti of Dartmouth College
and David Wise of the National Bureau of Economic Research.
In a paper entitled "Choice, Chance and Wealth Dispersion at
Retirement," they reported the findings of their study comparing the lifetime earnings of households with net worth at retirement. Not surprisingly, they found a number of households
with high lifetime earnings and little wealth at retirement.
Conversely, they found households with modest lifetime earn-

ings and a great deal of wealth at retirement. They then exam-
ined random events that could positively or negatively affect
household wealth, such as inheritance or poor health, to see
what impact they had. Here is what they concluded:

> We find that very little of this dispersion can be
> explained by chance in individual circumstances—"largely
> outside the control of individuals"—that might limit the
> resources from which saving might plausibly be made. . . .
>
> We conclude that the bulk of the dispersion must be
> attributed to differences in the amount that households
> choose to save. The differences in saving choices with sim-
> ilar lifetime income earnings lead to vastly different levels
> of asset accumulation by the time retirement age
> approaches.

Spendthrift Nation

The unwillingness to save is what keeps most of us in the
time/money trap. The American work ethic is fine, but the
American savings ethic is severely lacking.

A 1997 survey by Public Agenda of twelve hundred nonretired
Americans, aged twenty-two to sixty-one, revealed the following:

- Thirty-eight percent of baby boomers have saved less than
  $10,000.
- Thirty percent of those aged 51–61 have saved less than
  $10,000 and only 29% of those in this age bracket have
  accumulated at least $100,000.

—AMERICAN DEMOGRAPHICS, AUGUST 1997

Census Bureau data from 1995 revealed that the median savings of American families was only $1,000 when household debts and credit cards were subtracted. Without subtracting debts the median figure was $2,700. Most of us don't have a plan. We simply live from paycheck to paycheck.
—*The Arizona Republic,* October 20, 1999

Basically, about one-third of all households are broke. . . . Basically the problem is this—we've got a third of the population with no cash assets.
—Scott Burns, *The Dallas Morning News,* August 22, 1999

Only one third of Americans are saving enough for retirement. The net worth of the average American, exclusive of their home, is about $15,000. And half of all retirees over 65 would be living at poverty levels but for their Social Security checks.
—Paul Farrell, CBS.MarketWatch.com, August 31, 2000

Not including home equity, U.S. households had a median of only $9,850 in net financial assets in 1998 (latest year Fed data available). In 2000, the average household with at least one credit card carried a credit card balance of $8,000.
—*USA Today,* February 21, 2001

According to the Consumer Federation of America, fifty-three percent of Americans surveyed said that they live from paycheck to paycheck sometimes, most of the time or always. The percentage rose to 64 percent for households with moderate incomes of $20,000 to $50,000 a year and to 79 percent for those with low incomes of less than $20,000.
—Associated Press Online, February 20, 2001

I just saw a Yankelovich survey of the 18-to-34 set. It said that twice as many of them have considered applying for a slot on *Who Wants to Be a Millionaire* as have put money into an individual retirement account.

—FRED BARBASH, *THE WASHINGTON POST,* AUGUST 6, 2000

"Experts say seven out of ten lottery winners go through their winnings in three years."

—*NBC NIGHTLY NEWS,* AUGUST 27, 2001

Here's a simple question: Would you rather spend most of your life working for money or have money working for you? Most of us prefer the latter, but we do the former simply because we don't save enough. Every dollar you save and invest earns more dollars for you. Every dollar you spend doesn't. Every dollar you save and invest shortens the time between today and the day you reach the winner's circle. Every dollar you spend doesn't. And every dollar you carry in debt lengthens the time it will take you to reach financial freedom. You can't reach for the stars and dig a hole at the same time.

SAVING IS BETTER THAN EARNING

From a purely financial viewpoint, it's better to save money than to earn it, because you aren't taxed on what you don't earn. Every $1,000 you don't spend on expensive cars, clothing, jewelry, lavish vacations or eating in fancy restaurants means more than $1,400 you don't have to earn. Conversely, for every additional $1,000 you spend, you'll have to earn over $1,400 because you have to pay taxes, too. Income and spending are taxed, but wealth isn't. The only exception is the estate tax levied on the wealthy after both spouses are deceased. In fact, the government encourages saving through tax-deferred and tax-free savings programs such as 401(k) and Roth IRA.

Every enduring financial fortune is built on a foundation of saving. Earning isn't going to make you a fortune if you don't save. Inheriting millions isn't going to keep you wealthy if you don't save. Winning a big lottery won't help if you don't save. Investing will get you there, but you can't invest what you don't save. The road to financial freedom runs straight through the heart of Save City. There's no shortcut. There's no bypass. Show me a self-made millionaire and I'll show you a dedicated saver.

Are you and your spouse in the time/money trap? Are both of you working long hours to pay for a lifestyle you don't have the time to enjoy? Is there too much month at the end of the money? Are your bills stressing you out? Well, I have an important question for you: Have you considered spending less, saving more and just relaxing?

I know that I'm preaching heresy in our earn-to-spend society, but the problem is obvious. We're a nation of spendaholics. The marketing moguls have us convinced that spending is cool. Every day we are bombarded with thousands of ads telling us to spend, spend, spend. They do such a great job that most people confuse who they are with what they have. Lack of money isn't the problem; lack of saving is. In a world where saving can make you rich and free, most of us are held captive by our own spending habits. A survey by Partrick J. Purcell of 1998 Census Bureau data reports that 61% of all workers (sixty-six million people) between twenty-four and sixty-four have no retirement savings account of any kind.

Much of what happens to our money can't be controlled: We can't totally control how much we earn. We can't control how much we are taxed. We can't control the rate of inflation or the return on our investments. The single area where we have control over our money is in how much we choose to spend. You can't control the economy, but you can control your economy.

I've heard and read all the excuses about why people can't save: We are becoming a society of haves and have-nots; it takes two incomes to make it today; women and minorities can't save because they earn less; the next generation won't live as well as their parents. Baloney! One sure way to stay in the time/money trap is to convince yourself you can't save.

The truth is that every living, natural-born American citizen with an I.Q. above room temperature is a winner of the economic lottery. Through sheer luck, we live in the richest nation in the history of the world, and it's only going to get richer. The great American wealth train is on track and accelerating. Why sit alongside the tracks and let it pass you by when you can get on board and share in the wealth? Once you acquire the savings habit, your ticket is punched.

What a Country!

A 1995 study from the National Center for Policy Analysis found that Americans living at the poverty level owned more dishwashers than families in the Netherlands, Italy or the United Kingdom. The study also reported that our poor owned as many clothes dryers as the people of Sweden and more microwave ovens than any nation in Europe.

In their book, *Myths of Rich & Poor,* W. Michael Cox and Richard Alm point out that poor American households in 1994 compared very favorably to all American households in the early 1971 with respect to the trappings of middle-class life. Take a look at the following table.

EVEN THE POOR HAVE MORE THAN THEY USED TO

PERCENT OF HOUSEHOLDS WITH:	POOR HOUSEHOLDS 1994	ALL HOUSEHOLDS 1971
Washing machine	71.7	71.3
Clothes dryer	50.2	44.5
Dishwasher	19.6	18.8
Refrigerator	97.9	83.3
Freezer	28.6	32.2
Stove	97.7	87.0
Microwave	60.0	<1.0
Color television	92.5	43.3
Videocassette recorder	59.7	0
Personal computer	7.4	0
Telephone	76.7	93.0
Air conditioner	49.6	31.8
One or more cars	71.8	79.5

Source: W. Michael Cox and Richard Alm, *Myths of Rich & Poor* (New York: Basic Books, 1999), 15.

Please don't misunderstand me. I'm not saying that America's poor have a great life or that we should turn our back on them. We need to open their eyes to the economic possibilities and help them, primarily through education. But we also need to realize that the most you can ever give anyone is opportunity. Ultimately, we are all accountable for our own fate.

FINANCIAL FREEDOM IS FREE

Before you declare me insane, hear me out. Achieving financial freedom doesn't cost a dime. It isn't a gift and it isn't easy, but it's free. What costs money are all the things you buy, which prevent you from saving, investing and reaching the winner's circle. When you save money, you pay yourself. The more you pay yourself, the sooner you can buy your freedom and spend your life doing whatever you want.

With such an enormous payoff, why aren't more people committed to saving? One reason is not realizing that small savings compounded over time can be the difference between poverty and financial freedom. Another reason lies in an unwillingness to invest some of today's earnings to build a better tomorrow. But the third reason may be the biggest one of all: *We glorify spenders and ridicule savers.* Big spenders are portrayed as rich, successful, generous and popular. Savers are denigrated as penny-pinching, cheap, tight and miserly. For example:

- Jews throughout history have been falsely stereotyped as greedy because of their ability to save money. In truth, most are exceptionally generous and philanthropic. Millennia of persecution required them to save just to survive.
- Every holiday season children read, hear or watch Charles Dickens's classic *A Christmas Carol*. Who's the villain? Ebenezer Scrooge. His very name conjures up the image of a heartless, tightfisted businessman.
- According to Comedy Central's Ben Stein, "People who are frugal in Hollywood are generally considered freaks, losers and geeks. I really wish we could get a message out of Hollywood that saving is a very good thing to do."

In addition to demeaning thrift, movies and television regularly portray wealthy people and business owners as treacherous villains, such as the infamous J. R. Ewing in *Dallas*. It's common for university professors to depict businesspersons as greedy, dishonest and evil. Yet those businesspeople create the wealth that makes universities and faculty livelihoods possible.

Not surprisingly, in an American Association of Retired Persons survey of people over eighteen, one third said they don't want to be wealthy. Only 8% said it would take them $1 million or more to feel wealthy. Four out of five feared that wealth would make them greedy, and three fourths feared it would make them insensitive. While most of us would like to be millionaires, we don't want to be *like* millionaires.

Our nation is very ambivalent about wealth. Achieving economic success is the centerpiece of the American dream, but we frown on doing what it takes to achieve it and tend to distrust those who have it.

SAVING IS AS SIMPLE AS VST

Movie star Errol Flynn once remarked, "My problem lies in reconciling my gross habits with my net income." In the final analysis, you can do only two things with every dollar that comes into your life—spend it or save it. The key to living successfully with money lies in striking the right balance.

I recommend the VST approach to saving: vision, strategies, tactics. First, commit yourself to living the following vision: *I seek to get maximum lifetime enjoyment from the money that comes into my life*. That means getting to enjoy some of your money every day, including today. You might treat yourself to the good things in life, provide for your family, contribute to a charity or cause you strongly believe in, assist with your grandchildren's education—whatever your heart desires. It's your money, and it's yours to enjoy as you see fit.

However, unless your time is very short, it's impossible to maximize your lifetime enjoyment of money without saving a part of what you earn. That's why you need strategies and tactics for saving. Let's begin with the most well known:

1. *Pay yourself first.* At least the first 10% of every paycheck you earn goes to some form of saving. Those who wait until it's convenient to save wait forever. If achieving financial freedom is Job One, then saving is Financial Priority One. If you have no savings, accumulate six months' worth of living expenses in a savings or money-market account before you begin investing in index funds. That's your emergency fund.

2. *Start early.* The earlier you begin saving and investing, the more you'll compound and the sooner you'll reach the winner's circle.

Here's a good example to illustrate the value of starting early: Bob and Betty are both twenty-one years old. Bob invests nothing until age thirty-one and then begins investing $2,000 per year for thirty-four years for a total investment of $68,000. Betty invests $2,000 per year starting at age twenty-one for only ten years, for a total investment of $20,000. Assuming both their investments earn an average annual return of 10% Bob's portfolio will be worth $419,000 at age sixty-five. However, Betty's portfolio will be $814,000. By starting ten years earlier, Betty earned a payoff of $324,000 more than Bob's with only 29% of the investment.

3. *Consider devoting future pay raises and windfall incomes into saving and investing.* The more you save, the sooner you're out of the time/money trap. If you're serious about reaching the winner's circle early, you will probably have to save at least 30 to 50% of your income. The way to do that painlessly is to funnel future windfalls and salary increases into savings. Most people make the mistake of spending raises and windfalls on new luxuries. Once tasted, those luxuries have a way of becoming necessities, and the vicious cycle of earning to spend continues.

When I started my teaching career, I got some great advice from John Davidson, a faculty member at my alma mater. I had the option of getting my nine-month teaching salary in nine paychecks or twelve monthly paychecks spread out over the entire year. The rational financial thing to do was to get paid in nine pay-checks because I would get use of the money sooner. However, John said, "Michael, get your salary in twelve paychecks, because you'll get used to living at that level of income, and when you earn extra money teaching summer school, you can save and invest it." It was great advice. Whenever I taught summer school, received book royalties or additional income, a large part was devoted to saving and investing. That early-acquired habit went a long way toward making me financially independent.

4. *Defer that tax to the max.* Would you believe there are people who pass up the chance to earn a pay raise for no additional work and a legal tax shelter at the same time? If your business has an employer-sponsored, tax-deferred account such as a 401(k) and you aren't saving the maximum allowable by law, you're probably one of them. A survey by Scudder Kemper Investments revealed that only a third of workers in their twenties and thirties contribute the maximum to their 401(k). In effect, they pass up the tax savings from the income that would be sheltered, and they also forgo the typical company matching funds of 50 cents for each dollar the employee contributes up to 6% of pay.

Tax-deferred accounts, such as 401(k), 403(b), Keogh, SEP IRA and others, are outstanding ways to accumulate wealth. That money is tax-deductible; most employers kick in matching funds; it compounds tax-free; and the money isn't taxed until you begin withdrawing it, usually after age fifty-nine and a half. Check with your employer or, if you're self-employed, with your CPA or financial planner to find out which plan is best for you. Find out the maximum you can contribute each year and *do it*! This strategy and our next one are just too good to pass up.

5. *Don't be a sloth, do a Roth.* A Roth IRA is the other terrific way to accumulate wealth. The money you contribute to a Roth IRA isn't tax-deductible. That's the bad news. The very good news is that the money compounds tax-free and is never taxed. Withdrawing the money is tax-free. Unlike tax-deferred programs such as a 401(k), you don't have to begin withdrawals at age seventy and a half and can even pass it on to your heirs tax-free. Assuming the money in a Roth has been invested for at least five years, you can begin withdrawals as early as age fifty-nine and a half. However, you can withdraw money before then without incurring a penalty if the assets are used for the firsttime purchase of a home, with a lifetime limit of $10,000.

If you're under age fifty, the maximum you can contribute to a Roth IRA rises from $3,000 in years 2002, 2003 and 2004; to $4,000 in years 2005, 2006 and 2007; then to $5,000 in 2008. After 2008 contribution limits will be adjusted for inflation. People fifty and over can contribute $3,500 in 2002, 2003 and 2004; $4,500 in 2005; $5,000 in 2006 and 2007; and $6,000 in 2008. You must have earned income, and an adjusted gross income of under $95,000 if filing singly, or under $150,000 if filing jointly, to contribute the maximum amount. Married couples with an adjusted gross of over $160,000, and singles with an adjusted gross of over $110,000, are ineligible. Tax laws change over time, so check to see if you are eligible and contribute the maximum amount when you are.

6. *Driving can be hazardous to your wealth.* Other than the purchase of a home, cars are the highest-priced items most of us buy in a lifetime. But unlike homes, which tend to appreciate, new cars are a terrible investment, losing approximately one third of their value in the first two years. That new-car smell has to be one of the most expensive perfumes on the market when it comes packaged inside a new car.

From a financial standpoint, your best deal is to buy a two- to five-year-old car, pay cash and keep it as long as the maintenance and repair costs are reasonable. Forget about leasing unless you're bound and determined to own a new car every two or three years. Financially speaking, sport utility vehicles are the worst deal going. They cost about $20,000 more than the average car and consume copious amounts of fuel; you can count on spending another $100 to $250 a month for gas, maintenance and insurance. In case you're wondering, a onetime investment of that extra $20,000 in an index fund that returns 11% annually compounds to $1,300,017 in forty years.

The automobile is an integral part of American life, and buying a new car can be a wonderful experience. I've done it several times and no doubt will do it again. But you can be sure that there are millions of Americans living on Social Security today who spent potential multimillion-dollar retirement portfolios on the purchase of new cars throughout their working lives.

7. *Earn a guaranteed annual return of 18% the easy way.* Pay off your credit-card debt, because that's what the balance is likely costing you in interest. Don't kid yourself. Carrying a credit-card balance just adds more time to the years you spend in the time/money trap. If you carry a large balance, pay it off, because you won't get a guaranteed 18% return on your money anywhere else. Once the balance is paid, use credit cards for convenience and buy only what you can afford to pay cash for. Use only no-fee credit cards with at least a twenty-five-day grace period. If you can find one, choose a card that offers a rewards or rebate program. A good website for credit-card shopping is www.CardWeb.com.

8. *Document your spending.* Keep a spending log for one month, and you'll find all kinds of unnecessary expenditures that can be redirected toward achieving financial freedom. Carry a three-by-five card or small notepad wherever you go. Write down what you buy and how much each purchase costs. In addition to pointing out where your money goes, this log will make you pause to consider if an item is really worth buying. When you pay the monthly bills, add them to the spending log.

At the end of the month, total up the amount spent by item, and the numbers will likely surprise you. Are you spending too much on books (heaven forbid!), dining in fancy restaurants, fancy coffees, cocktails, software, clothes, jewelry? A lot of what we purchase are impulse items that add little or nothing to our enjoyment, and those are the items to cut back on or totally eliminate. Remember, just $8.25 a day funds a Roth IRA.

9. *Calculate the cost of lost wealth.* Are you driving your financial freedom? Are you wearing it on your wrist, on your fingers or around your neck? Are you eating it in fancy restaurants, smoking or drinking it? Are you giving it to your landlord by renting a posh apartment when you could be investing in a home that will appreciate and give you a handsome tax deduction? The true cost of an item isn't merely the out-of-pocket cost. It's the forgone wealth that money compounded over time can earn for you.

A good rule of thumb says that buying a midpriced used car lowers your average annual cost of driving about $2,500 a year, as opposed to buying a new car every three years. So, let's assume that instead of buying a new car every three years, you buy a three-year-old car and invest the $2,500 annual savings in a total stock-market index fund that averages an 11% annual return. If you do that starting at age twenty, by age sixty-five your car savings account grows to $2,466,596. Practice this habit in a two-car family and your net worth soars to $4,933,193 by age sixty-five. When your friends ask how you became a multi-millionaire, you can tell them you were in the used-car business.

In keeping with that theme, let's consider the lost wealth that buying certain items would cost you by age sixty-five, assuming that the money would have been invested in an index fund and earned slightly less than the stock-market average annual return of 11%. Take a look at the table.

WHAT SPENDING TODAY COSTS YOU TOMORROW

Item Purchased	Cost of Wealth Forgone at Age 65
$5,000 wristwatch at age 27	$263,781
$1 a day in lottery tickets starting at age 18	$579,945
$20,000 mink coat at age 35	$457,846
$10,000 diamond ring at age 25	$650,009
$1,440 annual interest charges on an average credit-card balance of $8,000 from age 21	$1,606,404
$5 a day on junk food, smoking and alcohol from age 21	$2,080,121
$25 a day in restaurants starting at age 21	$10,400,605
$1,000 monthly rent starting at age 21	$13,386,696

As you can see, the power of compound interest and the Rule of 72 have enormous leverage that can work for or against you. I'm not against owning the good things in life and enjoy quite a few of them myself. Just be aware of their true lifetime cost and decide if owning them now is worth delaying or denying your financial freedom.

10. *Realize that all debts are not created equal.* While debt is usually frowned on, it can be a good investment. Going into debt for a home, business or education can be an excellent investment, provided that we don't overextend ourselves and the cost of borrowing isn't excessive. For example, I consider the money I borrowed for graduate school one of the best investments I ever made. I carry a mortgage on our home because the combination of a low-interest-rate loan and tax-deductible interest virtually guarantees that I can make a higher long-term return by investing the money in a low-risk bond fund than I would by paying off the mortgage. But if I were borrowing the money at the double-digit rates of the early eighties, it would have been paid off long ago.

According to the late Will Rogers, "Too many people spend money they haven't earned, to buy things they don't want, to impress people they don't like." Just because someone lives in a big house, drives an expensive car and wears flashy jewelry doesn't mean he or she is rich; indeed, the poorhouse may be just one paycheck away. The difference between wealth and the trappings of wealth is as big as the difference between lightning and a lightning bug. The single greatest determining factor of whether you will become a have or a have-not is whether you choose to be a saver or a save-not.

INCREASE THE MARKET VALUE
OF YOUR TIME
INSTEAD OF WORKING LONG HOURS

You don't have to be the one who works the most hours, just the one who is most there during the hours you work.

—JAMES EVANS, CEO, BEST
WESTERN HOTELS

What's an hour of your time worth where you work? If you spend forty hours per week at the office and are paid $1,000 per week, the obvious answer is $25. But is that really accurate? What if it takes you an hour each day to commute to and from work? What if you put in another ten hours per week at home telecommuting and doing paperwork on work-related matters? You're really putting in a fifty-five-hour week under those conditions, which is quite typical in today's work world.

Let's consider your annual salary minus some rather typical expenses, as depicted in the following table.

YOUR REAL TAKE-HOME PAY

ITEM	AMOUNT
Salary	$52,000
Taxes	(14,000)
Commuting costs	(2,000)
Work clothes	(1,500)
Day care for two children	(10,400)
Net pay	**$24,100**

Now, let's assume you work 48 weeks per year, with 2 weeks paid vacation and 10 paid holidays. That means the total number of hours worked in a year is 48 × 55, or 2,640. Divide $24,100 by 2,640 hours and you learn that your take-home hourly wage is nowhere near $25. It's $9.13. That's a little over one third of what you thought it was.

If you need more money, what do you do? The good old American work ethic tells us that the way to get rich is to work longer and harder. And judging from the findings of the following surveys, that's exactly what most of us are doing. Consider:

- A 1999 Gallup poll found that 44% of all Americans consider themselves workaholics. That's over a hundred million people. Seventy-seven percent said they enjoy time away from the job more than they do time on the job.
- The July 2000 issue of *American Demographics* reports that the average married couple is working 717 hours more each year than a working couple in 1969.
- According to the National Sleep Foundation, we get about 20% less sleep than our ancestors did a hundred years ago. Forty-five percent of adults surveyed say they'll give up precious sleep time to get more work done.
- A survey by Office Team, a Menlo Park, California, national staffing firm, revealed that 19% of employees

work through their lunch hour every day. Forty-three percent skip lunch at least once a week.

- A Hilton Generational Time Survey of 1,220 adults reported:

  - 68% need more fun
  - 67% need a long vacation
  - 66% often feel stressed
  - 60% feel time is crunched
  - 51% want less work and more play
  - 49% feel pressured to succeed
  - 48% feel overwhelmed

Perhaps you're familiar with the old saying "The harder I work, the luckier I get." It's a beautiful thought, but when it comes to earning money, it simply isn't true. Money doesn't flow to hard work. Money flows to value. While you may have to work hard to create value, it isn't your hard work that attracts the money: It's the value. Nobody cares about the labor pains, but everybody wants to see the baby. Working hard without creating perceived value is as futile as a car spinning its wheels in mud.

If you want to earn more money, stop believing in the myth that working long hours is the answer. Instead, focus your time and energy on getting paid more for your time. The way to get paid more is to increase the perceived value of what you do.

As an employee, you increase your perceived value by convincing an employer or potential employer that what you bring to the business is worth much more than your paycheck. For example, winning head football coaches at big-time college programs earn far more than the chancellors and athletic directors they report to. That's because money flows to value. If the coach fields a consistent winner, every home game is a sellout, and the school reaps additional revenues from television appearances, bowl games, concessions and alumni contributions. The revenue from ticket sales of just one home game more than pays the coach's annual salary. If the university pays him millions and he fields a team that brings in tens of millions, the university has gotten a bargain. If the university balks at paying him the going rate, you can be sure that another college in desperate need of a winning coach will gladly hire him.

It's also common for top salespeople to earn more than the executives they report to because of the revenue they bring in. Executives with a track record of making money-losing businesses profitable are paid enormous sums. Top doctors, lawyers, software writers and product designers can practically name their price. Their results are worth more than the money they're paid.

A business creates perceived value by giving the customer the best deal for the money, as it's perceived. For example, customers who shop at Wal-Mart believe it's a great deal because the prices are so low. Customers who shop at Nordstrom believe it's a great deal because the product and service quality are so high. The former creates value as a low-cost provider, while the latter creates value with exemplary quality.

Most of us stay in the time/money trap because we work long hours and spend. The way to get out of the trap is to increase the market value of your time and to save. When it comes to earning money, the harder you work, the more tired you get. The more value you create, the richer you get.

WELCOME TO THE FREE-AGENT ECONOMY

In 1972 a father told his recently graduated son, "Never get married to a company, because no company is married to you." While that may have been good advice then, it's a truth worth carving in stone today. There was a time when loyal employees of large companies were virtually assured of employment until age sixty-five and a nice company pension after that. In today's economy, profitable businesses lay off between six and eight hundred thousand people each year. For most employees, "job security" is an oxymoron.

But despite the nostalgia for the good old days, a new way of doing business is providing us with more freedom, more opportunities to get rich and the potential to build a much better life. It just requires different expectations and a different way of looking at the world of work, because the rules have changed in three basic ways.

First, we should count on rampant, unpredictable change as routine and learn to thrive on it. The accelerating pace of technological progress has created a business environment where success is short-lived. New jobs are constantly created and dissolved. Today's new breakthrough product rapidly becomes obsolete. The Internet gives customers the ability to shop the world at the speed of light in search of the best deal—and they do. Your loyal customer today is someone else's tomorrow. Your job today may vanish tomorrow. Expect to have many jobs and several careers in your lifetime. It's the future. Learning how to adapt to and capitalize on change is counterintuitive but essential. This is covered in more detail in Choice 6.

Second, because job and career conditions can change rapidly and without warning, you need to think of yourself as being in business for yourself, regardless of your livelihood. You are the CEO of You, Inc. You're in charge of the production, marketing, research and development and finance divisions of your enterprise. It's your responsibility to have a marketable product and/or service that you can deliver flawlessly. You have to know how to sell yourself, create visibility and position what you sell as unique and special. You have to invest in learning new skills and sharpening old ones to boost your future value. Finally, You, Inc., has to earn a meaningful profit for the value you deliver.

Third, the big money nowadays goes to those who work with their brains and not with their hands. In the industrial age, people made things. In the information age, machines make things. Today, 80% of the U.S. workforce generates and processes information and provides services. That's because computers and robots do routine tasks much better, faster and cheaper than we do. In order to decrease costs, routine jobs are automated or performed by people in less developed nations where wage rates cost far less. Routine management, clerical and assembly-line jobs have a very bleak future. Creative problem solvers, innovators and knowledge workers have a great future.

KEYS TO BUILDING VALUE

Generally speaking, the amount of money you earn depends on:

- What you do
- How well you do it
- The difficulty of replacing you

Ideally, there is very high demand for what you do, you do it extremely well and you are so unique as to be virtually irreplaceable. In the real world your odds of achieving that are about the same as the odds of hitting a hole in one for eighteen straight holes in a round of golf. While you probably won't come anywhere close, you should strive for the best you can. With that thought in mind, here are some specific ideas for increasing your market value in today's economy:

1. *Focus on employability instead of job security.* Like it or not, the unwritten employment agreement between companies and employees has been broken. Always strive to do the best job possible for your current employer, but don't allow yourself to become totally dependent on one business. Even if a company or organization guarantees you lifelong employment, circumstances may deteriorate to the point where you want to leave. The key to thriving in today's economy is to have a well-honed set of marketable talents and skills that aren't dependent on any one employer or customer. The responsibility for acquiring, improving and updating those skills is totally yours.

Unless you're self-employed, the day will almost certainly come when you either want to or have to leave your current job. Be prepared and ready for it.

2. *Earning is rooted in learning.* Knowledge is the fertilizer that makes your money tree blossom. If you need more formal education to develop career skills, bite the bullet and get it. Another way to get the skills you need is by working for a company that will train you as part of your job or finance your formal education. Smart companies today realize that training and upgrading employee skills is an investment that pays off in attracting and improving the productivity of good people.

Devote one hour a day to learning skills that will enable you to achieve your lifetime goals. Never before in history have so many of us had so much knowledge at our fingertips. You can surf the Internet and instantly find almost any kind of information. It's better than having the Library of Congress on your desk. Carry books with you to read when you take the bus or train to work or while waiting for an appointment. Keep current by listening to cassette programs and CDs while you're driving, showering or exercising. If you're trying to save money, check out books from your local library. Nobody is too poor to learn. Benjamin Franklin's comment that "An investment in knowledge pays the best interest" is truer today than ever. In times of rapid change, the learners inherit the earth.

3. *Create a side income.* If you dream of being your own boss someday, start a business on the side and begin learning the skills you need. That's what I did, and it was my salvation. Creating a side income gives you more control over your earnings and decreases your vulnerability to layoffs, downsizing, office politics and bureaucrats. Initially it requires putting in longer hours, but if you have a marketable idea that makes good use of your talents, the long-term payoff can be an early trip to the winner's circle.

A Great Way to Find Out What You Need to Learn

Here's a simple, commonsense way to take years off your learning curve. If you want to become one of the best at what you do, talk to someone who already is. Ask him or her where to find the best sources of information and what skills are most important to master. Ask questions such as:

- What are the most valuable lessons you've learned about being successful?
- What was most helpful to you when you were learning the ropes?
- What are the biggest mistakes to avoid and the greatest obstacles to overcome?
- Whom would you recommend I talk with?
- What books and periodicals should I be reading?
- Are there any courses that I should take?
- Are there any professional associations I need to join?
- What do you do to stay up to date?
- If you could give only one piece of advice to someone who wanted to do what you do, what would it be?

It's been said that a person who wants to be rich should invite a rich person to dinner and pay for the meal. Successful people in almost every walk of life are usually accessible and willing to share much of what they know. All they ask is a sincere interest on your part and that you not take too much of their time. But one word of caution: Have the common courtesy to ask questions of someone other than a person you plan to compete with directly.

Learning allows you to profit from other people's experiences without incurring the pain. Whenever you can learn from other people's mistakes or good fortune, do so. Personal experience is a great teacher, but learning only from personal experience is for fools. So, when you're trying to master something new, ask those who do it best. They can direct you to the right sources, spare you from the pain of mistakes you would have made and you'll probably come away with an abundance of great new ideas—at little to no cost.

4. *Practice the Lagniappe principle.* Two hundred years ago, Creole shopkeepers in southern Louisiana practiced what they called "Lagniappe" (pronounced lan-yap). It means "something extra." If a customer placed an order for several items, the shopkeeper might throw in an extra item, such as a slab of bacon or a pound of coffee, at no charge. Or if the customer asked for five pounds of sugar, the shopkeeper would carefully scoop five pounds of sugar onto the scale. Then he would smile, add an extra scoop and say, "Lagniappe." It was his way of saying, "Because I appreciate your business, I'm giving you your money's worth and a little bit more." Like the baker's dozen, it's a great way to foster customer loyalty.

Lagniappe is also one of the best ways to increase your perceived value in the marketplace. Customers, bosses and companies are always looking for people who deliver more than they promise or are paid to do.

Make it a habit to find ways to pleasantly surprise your customers, colleagues and bosses by going the extra mile. Since most people do only what's required, doing more is one sure way to stand out from the crowd. Your reputation will quickly grow, your services will be in demand and you can charge more for your time. As Napoleon Hill wrote almost eighty years ago, "Make it your habit to render more service and better service than that for which you are paid, and lo! Before you realize what has happened, you will find that THE WORLD IS PAYING YOU FOR MORE THAN YOU DO."

5. *Build your brand.* As the CEO of You, Inc., you need to do more than good work. You need to create visibility, too. The world isn't going to beat a path to your door unless it knows you exist, what benefits you provide and what makes you special. That's what building your brand is all about.

Begin by describing what you do that builds value in as few words as possible. For example, I help people work smarter. The help comes in the form of books, articles, audio or video programs, speeches, seminars and consulting, but helping people to work smarter is the essence of what I do. There is a good market for that, and the business has been very good to me.

Your next job is to position yourself as unique and special. Look at your work through the eyes of those who hire you. What do they value most when they hire someone like you? What problems do they want you to solve? What can you do better than anyone else? Take the answers to those questions and write a short, original statement, phrase or word that tells people why you're the person they need. This is your unique sales proposition, or USP. Its purpose is to set you apart from those who do similar work. Here are some well-known USPs:

- Terminix: No bugs. No hassles.
- Hallmark: When you care enough to send the very best.
- Like a good neighbor, State Farm is there.
- Always low prices, always Wal-Mart.

Finally, build a brand by getting your name and message in front of those in charge of hiring. Volunteer to speak at a luncheon, participate in a panel discussion or conduct a free seminar. Write an article and publish it where those you can help will read it. See if you can get interviewed discussing your work on radio and TV. Write a book to demonstrate your command of your area of expertise. Volunteer to write a regular column for a newspaper or trade journal. Create a website and alert your potential buyers to its frequently updated information. Those are all excellent ways to create visibility and build your brand.

6. *Practice lateral loyalty.* Despite all the talk of workplace loyalty being dead today, it is very much alive. It's just different. Instead of flowing vertically between company and employee, loyalty flows laterally. The loyalty that matters today is loyalty to the project, your partners, the work, your customers and your community. Form partnerships that produce far better results than any of you could have produced individually. Work on improving your "soft" skills as a communicator and team player. Once you become known as a supportive colleague, a great teammate and someone who does excellent work, your services will be in high demand.

7. *Be a practical imagineer.* All great fortunes begin with a great idea. Most of us use our brains to memorize, pay attention, observe and follow directions. Yet your brain's most potentially profitable use is to come up with great new ideas. We all have creative ability, and the more we use it, the better it gets. Creating a great new product or service puts you one step ahead of the competition in a rapidly changing world. Don't compete; create. Always be on the lookout for an idea from another industry that can be adapted to yours. Try to look at things from a different point of view. Question the status quo and challenge assumptions. People who generate profitable ideas are always in demand and handsomely paid.

8. *Use feedback as a basis for improvement.* In my book *How to Win Customers and Keep Them for Life,* I advise companies to get in the habit of asking their customers the Platinum Questions: How are we doing? And how can we get better?

Finding the answers to those two questions tells you how customers perceive the value of what you do and what you can do to increase that perception. That's very important information, because relative perceived quality is the single greatest key to long-term profitability. If this is important information for a business, it's critical information for You, Inc. Find out how you're doing in the eyes of your boss, your colleagues and your customers. Ask them, "How am I doing?" and "How can I get better?" Ask for specific ideas on what you can do or what you need to improve on. Good feedback from people you know, respect and trust can point the way to personal and professional growth.

9. *Know your value and don't be afraid to leave a job.* Today's economy rewards mobility more than loyalty. Give the job or the company where you work your very best. When you know you're ready for bigger assignments, odds are you'll be able to find them either where you work or somewhere close by. Network with colleagues and let everyone know that you're always on the market and eager to work for those who appreciate the value you create. Delivering true value in your current job will motivate your current boss to pay what it takes to keep you.

Finally, remember that finding a job is always easier when you have a job. If someone wants to hire you away from your current job, don't be afraid to ask for the best pay and benefits package you can get—including a good severance package. You'll never be in a greater position to negotiate.

In summary, money flows to value. Provide a product or service that a lot of people want. Do it extremely well. Do it so uniquely that you seem virtually irreplaceable. Give people their money's worth and then some. Those are the keys to increasing the market value of your time. The Rule of 72 applies to earnings, too. Increasing your income by just 10% a year doubles it in 7.2 years.

DO LESS BETTER INSTEAD OF TRYING TO DO IT ALL

Winners focus, losers spray.

—SIDNEY HARRIS

A Time-management Parable

—Author Unknown

A time-management expert was speaking to a class of ambitious young business students. To drive home a point, he used an illustration they will never forget. Standing in front of the group, he said, "Okay, time for a quiz." He pulled out a one-gallon, wide-mouthed jar and set it on a table in front of him. Then he produced about a dozen fist-sized rocks and carefully placed them, one at a time, into the jar.

When the jar was filled to the top and no more rocks would fit inside, he asked, "Is this jar full?" Everyone in the class said, "Yes." Then he said, "Really?" He reached under the table and pulled out a bucket of gravel. Then he dumped some gravel in and shook the jar, causing pieces of gravel to work themselves down into the spaces between the big rocks.

Then he asked the group once more, "Is the jar full?" By this time the class was on to him. "Probably not," one of them answered. "Good!" he replied. He reached under the table and brought out a bucket of sand. He started dumping the sand in, and it went into all the spaces left between the rocks and the gravel. Once more he asked the question: "Is this jar full?"

"No!" the class shouted. Once again he said, "Good!" Then he grabbed a pitcher of water and began to pour it in until the jar was filled to the brim.

Then he looked up at the class and asked, "What is the point of this illustration?" One eager beaver raised his hand and said, "The point is, no matter how full your schedule is, if you try really hard, you can always fit some more things into it!"

"No," the speaker replied, "that's not the point. The truth this illustration teaches us is: If you don't put the big rocks in first, you'll never get them in at all."

What are the "big rocks" in your life? A project that *you* want to accomplish? Time with your loved ones? Your faith, your education, your finances? A cause? Teaching or mentoring others? Remember to put these *big rocks* in first or you'll never get them in at all.

So, tonight or in the morning when you are reflecting on this short story, ask yourself this question: What are the "big rocks" in my life or business? Then put those in your jar first.

Time management is *the* critical skill for effective living. As the great management writer Peter Drucker pointed out, "Time is basic; unless it is managed, nothing else can be managed."

Despite all the books, tapes and seminars on the topic, the key to making good use of your time consists of just three simple steps:

- Decide what's most important.
- Set goals and priorities to do what's most important first.

- Develop good habits to do what's most important most efficiently.

It doesn't matter if you're a student, an employee, a small-business owner or a Fortune-500 CEO. It doesn't matter whether you're talking about an hour, a day, a week, a year or a lifetime. It doesn't matter how much you have to do and how little time you have to do it. If you habitually practice these three simple steps, you'll make excellent use of your time.

In Choice 1, you learned how to set lifetime goals: the big rocks in your life and the first step. You also learned how to set intermediate goals and write a project plan to help you achieve one or more of your lifetime goals; that's the second step. The final step is to learn the techniques for achieving those goals efficiently without feeling hassled, rushed or constrained. We will get to that shortly. But before we consider the "how," let's answer a very important "why."

WHY ARE SO MANY OF US
SO PRESSED FOR TIME?

The short answer is because we try to do too much and spread ourselves too thin. A number of major changes have converged to create a world where we perceive time as *the* scarce resource.

First, there is women's changing role in society. In earlier days, men's and women's roles were well defined: Dad was the wage earner and Mom the homemaker. Today's women are wage earners, homemakers, soccer moms, cooks, community volunteers and a litany of other things. All those roles compete for time and energy. As one time-starved corporate executive jokingly told her husband, "We sure could use a wife."

Another change has been corporate restructuring, where the workforce has been downsized and the workload hasn't. Those left to do the work have to put in longer hours to get it done.

A third major change is the blurring of the line between work and the rest of our lives. Thanks largely to technology, the distinction between work time and nonwork time is much less clear. More of us are working from home with every passing year. Cell phones, beepers, digital assistants, voice mail and laptop computers keep us continuously on tap for those who need to reach us. Welcome to the workday that never ends.

Finally, a free-agent economy is emerging. Work comes without a guaranteed future income. This creates a "make money while you can" mentality. Sure, you want to see your daughter in the school play or attend your son's ball game. But you've been offered an incredible amount of money to work on a project out of town for the next two weeks. It's just too good to turn down; it could lead to more work, and another opportunity this good may not come along for a long time.

Yet one overwhelming truth still remains: *None of these changes and circumstances can enter your life without your permission.* All the roles you feel compelled to fill are there because you chose them. All the things you have to get done are there because you agreed to do them. All the high-tech gadgets that make you always available are there because you allow them. All of your long hours at work are put in with your cooperation. With all the economic, societal and technological changes, it's still a free country. In the final analysis, how you choose to spend your time is up to you.

THE TRUTH ABOUT TIME MANAGEMENT

Time is totally unmanageable and uncontrollable. It plods along at the same unfaltering pace of 24 hours a day, 7 days a week, 365 days a year, regardless of what we do. What we call time management is really self-management.

The paradox of time is that nobody has enough but everybody has all there is. While life is unfair about many things, it's unquestionably fair when it comes to the amount of time in a day. We all get the same twenty-four hours.

There's a paradox in self-management, too: *The way to get more done is to do less better.* The more you try to be all things to all people, the greater are the odds you'll end up being nobody to everybody. The more things you try to do, the less likely you are to do any of them extremely well. Don't scatter your efforts like buckshot. Concentrate them and be a big gun. Remember the 80/20 Rule and invest the bulk of your time in the few activities with the highest payoffs.

TWO TRAPS TO AVOID

Let's assume you've made the commitment to invest your time actively. You've decided what's most important and are working to achieve your lifetime goals. In the shuffle of daily activities, you need to be alert for two potential pitfalls that could cost you dearly.

Trap #1—Confusing activity with productivity. There's an enormous difference between being busy and getting results. People have a tendency to be busiest when they are least secure about what they should be doing. An old saying from the French Foreign Legion advises, "When in doubt, gallop."

It used to amaze me in my university teaching days that those who were in their offices late at night or busily rushing from meeting to meeting were perceived as highly productive. One semester I shared an office with a faculty member who came in every day at nine A.M. and didn't leave the office until nine P.M. Many considered him a dedicated scholar simply because he put in a lot of face time. In fact, he spent most of that time poring over the stock-market pages of *The Wall Street Journal*, trying to pick hot stocks for his portfolio. As Laurence Peter told us, "An ounce of image is worth a pound of performance."

Focus on getting results, and make it your business to work for people who reward you for that. If your boss rewards you for working long hours or being busy, you've got the wrong boss.

Trap #2—Confusing urgency with importance. Every day we have things to do and things that happen. Some are urgent. Some are important. Some are both and some are neither. Here's what's very important to remember: *Urgent things are seldom important, and important things are seldom urgent.* When we confuse the two, we end up responding to everything like it's important, and what's truly important gets ignored.

Speeding to get to a luncheon appointment on time is urgent; getting there safely is important. Rushing to finish a job under a tight deadline is urgent; doing a quality job is important. Working endless hours to get your career or your business off the ground is urgent; taking the time to exercise, eat properly and get enough rest is important. Making the sale is urgent; building a business on great service and repeat customers is important. Feeling compelled to own that hot new sports car or take an expensive vacation is urgent; saving and investing to get to the winner's circle is important.

Responding to the tyranny of the urgent is a sure-fire recipe for less wealth and more stress. It's a key reason why so many of us are in the time/money trap. We passively allow what's urgent to dictate how our time and money are spent, while the less urgent and more important items get neglected.

Sooner or later, unattended important items become urgent. They're called crises. Health crises. Money crises. Family crises. Business crises. Most can be prevented with a little planning, forethought and preventive action. Problems rarely rise to the crisis level without warning. Choose to spend your time doing what's really important, and shield yourself from urgent but unimportant distractions. As President Dwight Eisenhower warned, "The more important an item, the less likely it is urgent, and the more urgent an item, the less likely it is important."

HOW TO DO LESS BETTER AND GET MORE DONE

People who reach the winner's circle don't work harder. They work smarter. Success doesn't hinge on how much you work, it depends on how intelligently you work. Making effective use of your time isn't compulsively running around with a stopwatch. Rather, it's a way of managing your life to achieve fulfillment and personal freedom.

Before you can improve your use of time, you have to know how you're currently spending it. Begin by keeping a time log for a week or two. It doesn't have to be anything elaborate or fancy. Just write down every activity, the time you begin, the time you end and how much time it takes. If you make a phone call, write down the beginning and ending times. Do the same when you check your e-mail, go to lunch, have a drop-in visitor, commute home and so on.

At the end of the week, total up how much time you spent on various activities. How much time did you spend on the telephone, in your car, seeing visitors, commuting, in meetings, answering your e-mail and so on? You will soon notice that most time usage is habit. We all tend to repeat certain activities that take a certain amount of time each day. Some are a good use of time, while others tend to waste it. Most of us think we know how our time is spent. In truth, most of us don't until we document it.

Once your time log is complete, look at the data you've compiled and write down the answers to the following questions:

- What are my three greatest time wasters?
- How much of my time is consumed by needless interruptions? How can they be minimized?

- What am I doing that's urgent and unimportant? How can these activities be reduced or eliminated?
- What are my most and least productive days and time of day?
- Whom do I need to spend more time with? Whom do I need to see less of?
- What activities should I be investing more time in?
- What can be eliminated or delegated?
- Am I trying to do too much?
- What habits or tendencies are causing me to waste time?
- How much time am I devoting to the achievement of my most important goals?

With the time-log results, the answers to those questions and your most important goals, you now have a clear road map to make better use of your time. The following strategies will help you toward that end.

1. *Have a daily quiet time for reflection and planning.* Novelist Victor Hugo wrote, "He who every morning plans the transaction of the day and follows out that plan, carries a thread that will guide him through the labyrinth of the most busy life." Every hour spent in planning is worth three in execution. Spend the first part of the day reviewing your goals, what you need to do and what you've gotten done. Your quiet time can be as short as a few minutes a day, but you need it to keep you focused on what's most important. During this time, make a daily to-do list like Charles Schwab did. It's a simple but powerful tool.

2. *Carve out large blocks of time to work on important activities.* Hoping that you will someday find the time to do what's important is an exercise in self-delusion. "Someday" is not a day of the week. The only way to find time is to eliminate other activities. If you're a writer, you need to schedule blocks of time for writing. If you're a salesperson, you need to spend a large part of your day in front of the customer. If you're a physician, you need to spend a lot of time seeing patients. Make sure the bulk of your time is spent on high-payoff activities.

3. *Make the most of prime time.* That's the time of day when you're at your best at doing a particular task. Take the most important item on your to-do list and schedule time to work on it when you're at your best. That way you give your best self to your most important work. If the job is one that requires solitude and concentration, schedule it for the morning, if that's when your thinking is best. If the job involves interacting with others, try to schedule it when you feel most sociable. Schedule less important and routine tasks during nonprime time when your energy level isn't as high.

4. *Say no to the unessential.* It's been said that stress is that feeling you get when your gut says no and your mouth says "I'd love to." Politely refuse all requests that prevent you from spending time on what's important. You don't have to please everyone. It's your right to say, "I can't do that for you because I already have too much to do." Offer to help at another time, if it's appropriate, or recommend someone who may be able to help.

5. *Keep a loose schedule with a backup plan.* Few days will go exactly as planned, and almost everything takes longer than we expect. A tight schedule is a recipe for feeling frustrated and harried. Allow for the unexpected by never scheduling more than half your time. Be prepared for delays and canceled appointments by having a Plan B. Bring along reading material or your laptop to work on other projects when you suddenly have a bonus of unexpected time.

6. *Attack important jobs with a single-minded focus.* Some people believe that being a good time manager consists of doing several things at once. We all see people who drive, put on makeup and talk on their cell phone simultaneously. That's a very negligent practice when you consider that safe driving is a life-and-death matter. Any important activity deserves your undivided attention.

Mindless routine activities are fine for multitasking. You can listen to tapes and take your dog for a run simultaneously. While watching TV you can check your e-mail, surf the Web or exercise. But for an important task that requires your concentration, focus on doing that one thing and do it to completion.

7. *Automate as many clerical, repetitive and trivial tasks as you can.* Set up your monthly bills to be automatically deducted from your checking account. Have your paycheck automatically deposited in your checking account. Establish an automatic purchase plan to buy index funds every month. Anything that can be automated is one less thing you have to do.

8. *Delegate everything but genius.* Whatever you do for a living has a core competency. Your unique combination of knowledge, talent and ability is what creates your value in the marketplace. Identify that and spend your work time developing it, improving it and doing it, then delegate everything else. Trying to do everything yourself just means less time for you to work on the high-value activities. Pay someone else to do the low-value activities and devote your time to doing what you do best.

When I moved out of an apartment and bought my first house, someone said, "Now you're going to have to cut the grass." That was in 1975, and I haven't purchased a lawn mower yet. Like many people, I hire someone who specializes in lawn care while I specialize in doing what I do best. That's what delegating is all about.

Similarly, don't drive clear across town just to save a few bucks. What is your time worth? While I strongly believe in saving, I also believe in spending money to free your time for more important activities.

9. *Conquer the clutter.* All clutter is caused by delayed decision making. It's true of cluttered desktops, overstuffed drawers, closets filled to the brim and garages overloaded with junk. Force yourself to make quick decisions, and clutter won't accumulate.

A person with a cluttered desktop spends an average of approximately one and a half hours per day looking for items or being distracted by what's on the desktop. Try to handle each piece of paper only once. Every time you pick up a piece of paper, resolve to either throw it away, file it or act on it and move it on its way.

Go through your closets, desktop and drawers, file cabinets, closets, attic, basement or anywhere you have clutter. Consider each item and ask yourself, "What's the worst thing that will happen if I get rid of this?" If it isn't too bad, dump it. Donate useful items such as clothing, old computers and furniture to local charities and get a nice tax deduction. Any item you haven't used in the past two years will probably never be used again, so ditch it. Consider this: If you spend just ten minutes a day looking for misplaced or lost items, you waste over sixty hours a year. Clutter is a time killer. Less is more.

10. *Take steps to block interruptions.* All that time you block out to do what's important will be severely diluted unless you take steps to keep from being interrupted. If you work in an office, close your door for part of the day so you can work undisturbed. While being available is important, being effective is more important. Let people know you're open to visits at certain times of the day and encourage them to meet with you then. Take the same approach to telephone calls. Let your voice mail or secretary take messages and allocate a portion of your day for placing and returning calls. Avoid meetings like the plague, if you can. Most meetings are a veiled attempt to avoid work and decision making.

If you find yourself frequently interrupted by crises, you need to take preventive action. At least 80% of all crises are preventable. Keep a log. When a crisis occurs, write down what it was, why it happened, how it was resolved and what can be done to keep it from recurring. You'll prevent many future crises and you'll have plans to quickly resolve the ones you can't avoid.

11. *Be the master of your telecommunications tools instead of their slave.* Technology is a two-edged sword. The positive edge is that you can work anywhere, anytime, and boost your productivity enormously. The negative edge is that left unchecked, it allows work to take over your entire life. Restaurants and theaters routinely ask people to turn off their cell phones and pagers. Some people in health clubs take their cell phones, covered in plastic sheaths, into the shower. Golfers regularly take calls from the office and check their investments from the fairway. The ability to work anywhere, anytime, too often becomes working everywhere all the time.

Never being able to get away from work is bad for your work and the rest of your life. You need time away to recharge your batteries and get a fresh perspective. Microsoft, the giant technology leader, encourages their employees to take "Think Days" to read a book or do some nonwork-related activities to gain a new perspective and prevent burnout.

Set boundaries around important activities and keep technology out. There's a time to be plugged in and a time to be unplugged. Make a clear distinction between work time and nonwork time. Turn off all the gadgets when you don't want to be disturbed. I once saw a sign that said, "Dogs come when they are called. Cats take a message and get back to you." Be a cat.

12. Frequently ask yourself, "What's the best use of my time and energy right now?" Answering this question several times a day will keep you focused on what's important and what you need to do now. Maybe it's taking a nap or vacation or doing nothing. Maybe it's working on an important project you've been putting off. Maybe it's spending more time with your family and friends. Just ask the question and you'll usually have a ready answer.

13. Never take time for granted. It's your most precious resource. All the money in the world can't buy back a moment. Some time ago I ran across the following item that makes the point beautifully. You may want to copy it and put it on your desk or your wall as a reminder.

The Value of Time

—AUTHOR UNKNOWN

Imagine there is a bank that credits your account each morning with $86,400.

It carries over no balance from day to day, allows you to keep no cash balance and, every evening, cancels whatever part of the amount you failed to use during the day.

What would you do? Draw out every cent, of course!

Well, everyone has such a bank. Its name is TIME. Every morning, it credits you with 86,400 seconds. Every night it writes off, as lost, whatever of this you have failed to invest to good purpose. It carries over no balance, and it allows no overdraft. Each day it opens a new account for you. Each night it burns the records of the day. If you fail to use the day's deposits, the loss is yours. There is no going back. There is no drawing against the tomorrow. You must live in the present, on today's deposits. Invest it so as to get from it the utmost in health, happiness and success. The clock is running. Make the most of today.

To realize the value of one year:
Ask a student who has failed a final exam.

To realize the value of one month:
Ask a mother who has given birth to a premature baby.

To realize the value of one week:
Ask an editor of a weekly newspaper.

To realize the value of one hour:
Ask lovers who are waiting to meet.

To realize the value of one minute:
Ask someone who has missed a train, bus or plane.

To realize the value of one second:
Ask someone who has survived an accident.

To realize the value of one millisecond:
Ask someone who has won a silver medal in the Olympics.

Yesterday is history
Tomorrow is a mystery
Today is a gift
That's why it's called the present!

Treasure every moment that you have! And treasure it more because you shared it with someone special, special enough to have your time . . . and remember time waits for no one.

Yesterday is a canceled check
Tomorrow is a promissory note
Today is cash on hand . . . Spend it wisely!

CAPITALIZE ON THE UNEXPECTED
INSTEAD OF BEING DERAILED BY IT

The biggest returns in life are on tenacity and flexibility.
Financial cleverness is barely in the race.

—SCOTT BURNS,

FINANCIAL COLUMNIST,

THE DALLAS MORNING NEWS

Life is full of pleasant and unpleasant surprises. Nobody likes being fired, downsized, losing a key customer, product failures or being forced out of business. Yet these things happen every day. Unexpected change is part of life. Even the most positive change involves some loss, and that's why we instinctively resist it. But should we?

I once had a telephone conversation with the cofounder of a large, international public-seminar company. When I asked him why he started the business, he replied, "Well, I went to work for a seminar company and got fired. Then I went to work for another seminar company and got fired. I figured I wasn't cut out to work for other people, so my partner and I started our own company." A few years after that conversation, the company was sold for many millions of dollars, making him a very wealthy young man.

Many self-made millionaires are former employees who became entrepreneurs. Gather a group of successful business owners together to reflect on their past and you're sure to hear several say that getting fired was one of the best things that ever happened to them. It hurt and made them angry. It motivated them to work hard, be successful and never let others control their future again.

Unfortunately, they're the exception and not the rule. The first thing that most people do after losing a job is file for unemployment. Then they find another job doing the same old kind of work in the same old way and remain in the same old trap. They refuse to think outside the box. Life hands them a "get out of jail free" card and they throw it away.

Winners, on the other hand, are masters at the art of serendipity. When the unexpected happens, no matter how unpleasant, they look for ways to capitalize on it. They know that every setback contains seeds of new and greater heights of success if they're persistent enough to look for them and follow through. Instead of feeling victimized and letting setbacks derail their plans, their attitude is "It's not over until I win." And because of that persistent, positive attitude, they do win.

Did you know that:

- Coca-Cola was a headache remedy that didn't work?
- Toll House cookies were invented by a lazy person who didn't want to grate chocolate and used chunks instead?
- The first Levi's jeans were made from leftover tent material that didn't sell?
- Post-it notes evolved from a failed experiment with new glues?
- The first Life Savers were created when the mint press malfunctioned and stamped out peppermint rings?

- Seventeen major New York publishers passed up the chance to publish a collection of short stories entitled "Chicken Soup for the Soul"?

Think of the fortunes that never would have materialized had the innovators given up when these setbacks occurred. But in every case, someone found a way to turn a negative event into a positive breakthrough. It's the broken eggs that make the omelet.

THE WINNER'S EDGE

Native intelligence, talent and education will all stack the odds of reaching the winner's circle in your favor. But the critical ingredient to achieving any major long-term goal is a positive, persistent attitude. Everyone's journey to the winner's circle is filled with obstacles. There are no exceptions. Obstacles are like death, taxes and presbyopia—you can count on them. You'll be given plenty of opportunities, distractions and temptations to abandon your goal and quit.

We all have mountains to climb, and some are larger than others. In the grand scheme of things, the size of the mountains is relatively unimportant; what *is* important is the way you perceive and react to them. People who react negatively think, "That's just my luck. I knew it was too good to be true. It's just not in the cards for me. People are against me. I can't do it." As a result, they throw up their hands, abandon their goal and guarantee failure. It's like basketball—you miss 100% of the shots you don't take.

But winners see obstacles in a totally different light. When confronted with a mountain, they immediately start making plans to make the most of it. Their thinking tends to go like this: "Can I go over, around or under it? Can I tunnel through it? Can I leverage it to create a shorter route to the winner's circle?

What's the opportunity here? Who can I call to get some ideas on how to handle this? What can I learn from this that will move me closer to the winner's circle? Some good can come from everything, including this, and I'm going to find it."

Winners know that big-time success is rooted in dogged persistence, and the key to persistence is faith. When you believe you can achieve a goal, you keep trying. And if you try hard enough and long enough, you will almost surely accomplish it. Those with the staying power to hold on against all odds and pursue their dreams with undying determination are ultimately life's big winners.

Research at the University of Kansas confirms that success hinges largely on believing in your ability to define your goals and seeing yourself as someone who can find pathways and motivation to achieve them. That's what Professor C. R. (Rick) Snyder defines as hope. This isn't the wishful-thinking kind of hope, as in "I hope I win the lottery." Nor is it blind optimism. Rather, it has to do with how strongly you believe in your own ability to set goals and achieve them.

Snyder created a scale that measures this particular brand of hope in individuals. According to Snyder, the Hope Scale predicts college success more accurately than SAT or ACT scores. Athletes who score high on the Hope Scale outperform low-hope competitors. People with high-hope scores tolerate pain and recover from illnesses faster than those with low hope.

Snyder's research seems to confirm what many self-help authors have been preaching for years: Life is largely a self-fulfilling prophecy. The results we get tend to reflect our expectations. If you don't expect much, you aim low, don't try too hard and don't get much. If you expect a lot, you aim high, work hard and get a lot. When you choose to believe you're a victim and the world is against you, you sabotage your own chances for success. When you believe you can do it, that the forces of God and humanity are with you, you get it done.

Winners, above all, see themselves as winners. The more we learn, the more it seems that the old cliché about the little engine that could may hold the ultimate key to success.

EXPECT THE UNEXPECTED AND THRIVE ON IT

One of the greatest lessons you'll ever learn is that life is full of second chances. But second chances often come disguised as unexpected and unwelcome events. If you look back on your own life, you'll probably be able to recall several examples when what you thought was the worst change that could happen turned out to be the best.

In a world where the rate of change is accelerating, it isn't enough to just tolerate change or learn to manage it. You need to anticipate it, embrace it, sometimes initiate it and learn to enjoy it. All change is initially uncomfortable and requires risk, but the more things change, the more opportunities and experiences you have. People who complain about the turbulent times we live in fail to realize that the turbulence creates opportunities to learn, to grow and to get rich. Practice the following techniques to help you ride the waves of change to the winner's circle:

1. *Keep your eyes on the prize.* If your long-term goal is to reach the winner's circle, don't allow unexpected events to cause you to abandon it. There are many possible roads to financial freedom, and you need to find only one. Take the case of Steve.

A graduate electrical engineer, Steve went to work for IBM with dreams of rising up the corporate ladder. But one day he read a very revealing article about height discrimination in the selection of corporate executives. Steve is five feet, seven inches tall. According to the study, 30% of all men but only 3% of corporate executives are five feet, seven inches or less. Not liking those odds, Steve asked to be demoted from engineer to engineering technician, where he would be paid an hourly wage rather than an annual salary. By doing this and working overtime, he increased his income significantly. He lived on a third of his pay, saved and invested another third and paid taxes with the final third. When his investments grew to ten times his annual pay, Steve quit IBM at the ripe old age of forty and moved from upstate New York to sunny Arizona, where he now works part-time at a job he enjoys.

2. *Don't be afraid of success.* One night my wife, Elke, asked if I would speak with her friend on the telephone. Mary (not her real name) had been offered a terrific job that was well suited to her background, experience and talents. The pay and perks were good, but Mary was terrified to leave her old job and wanted my advice. Before she could tell me anything about the job offer, I picked up the phone and said, "Mary, I'm going to ask you one question. If you weren't afraid, would you take the job?"

"Yes, I probably would," she tearfully replied.

"Then take the job," I said. "There's nothing wrong with being afraid. If I were in your shoes, I'd be scared, too. But you can't allow fear to control your life." She took the job and found it much more to her liking than the one she left.

If you are offered a wonderful opportunity requiring great change, don't let fear be the decision maker. Ask yourself, "What's the worst that can happen and can I live with it?" and "If I weren't afraid, would I seize this opportunity?" If the answer to both questions is yes, go for it. As playwright Neil Simon once remarked, "If no one ever took risks, Michelangelo would have painted the Sistine floor."

3. *Use disappointments as an incentive to spur you on to even greater success.* Unexpected setbacks hurt. Don't deny your feelings. Give yourself a brief time to grieve, then get back to work.

In 1983 I applied for a sabbatical leave from teaching. I

wrote in my application that I wanted to research and write about the relationship between performance and rewards in organizations. This topic interested me very much because I could see no relationship between the two at the university where I taught. The administration rejected my application, saying that my proposal was "lacking in quality." That bureaucratic comment ticked me off. I remember thinking to myself, "Lacking in quality, huh? I'll show them. I'm going to write the best book on the subject that I can." The book, *The Greatest Management Principle in the World,* was published in 1985, translated into over a dozen languages, adapted to produce several audio and video training programs and garnered a lot of speaking engagements. The book had a big write-up in *Success* magazine, and I was interviewed on ABC-TV's *Good Morning America.* The money I made from that book enabled me to take a two-year leave of absence without pay, which was four times longer than the sabbatical that I had applied for. During that time I wrote *How to Win Customers and Keep Them for Life,* which was extremely profitable. The success of those two books landed me in the winner's circle and funded an early university retirement far beyond my wildest dreams.

4. *Don't let other people's opinions limit your success.* You know your own capabilities far better than anyone else. An expert is just a person who knows all the reasons why you can't do something. For example, here are some expert opinions you may find interesting:

- Michael Jordan failed to make his high school basketball team as a sophomore.
- Following a young actor's first screen test, a memo from the MGM casting director read, "Can't act. Slightly bald. Can dance a little." That young actor was Fred Astaire.
- An expert once said of the legendary coach Vince Lombardi, "He possesses minimal football knowledge. Lacks motivation."

- A newspaper fired Walt Disney for lacking ideas.
- Ludwig von Beethoven played the violin awkwardly and preferred playing his own compositions. His teacher declared him hopeless as a composer.
- As a boy, Albert Einstein had trouble memorizing facts and was expelled from school. He later failed an entrance examination to study as an electrical engineer. After graduating as a teacher of mathematics and physics, he was unable to secure a teaching position because his professors felt him unworthy and failed to recommend him.

Stop for a moment and consider what the world would have missed if Michael Jordan, Fred Astaire, Vince Lombardi, Walt Disney, Ludwig von Beethoven and Albert Einstein had allowed others to define their capabilities. Every one of these people achieved legendary greatness, and every one was told he didn't have what it takes. If it's your dream and you have the passion to commit your time and effort, don't let anyone tell you it can't be done.

Instead of listening to critics, surround yourself with positive, upbeat people who believe in you and your dreams. Form a group of like-minded people who share similar dreams. Support groups are an excellent way to exchange ideas, provide encouragement and celebrate the good times. Surrounding yourself with the right people multiplies the joys of success and divides the burdens.

5. *Remember that every time one door closes, another door opens.* That was a favorite saying of my late literary agent, Arthur Pine, who wrote a wonderful book on the subject. Artie was one of the most encouraging people I have ever known. I'm sure he was a tough negotiator with publishers, but he was instantly likable and had a smile that could melt a glacier. Perhaps his finest work was the mentoring of his son, Richard, who is one of the top literary agents in the business.

In his book *One Door Closes, Another Door Opens,* Artie points out that setbacks don't just happen. They happen for a purpose. Doors close every day, yet we see people who open new doors and go on to greater levels of success. They don't dwell on the closed door. Instead, they look for an open one. If they find a door that's closed, they knock, or kick it open if need be. If they can't find a door, they build one. We all get knocked down. The key to success is to get back up and keep going. Artie's book is filled with inspiring stories of celebrities, authors and people from all walks of life who turned their setbacks into comebacks. Although it's out of print, there are still copies available, and it's a wonderful, inspirational read.

The Million-dollar Death Sentence

Diagnosed with emphysema at age forty-one, Ted Isaac was told by doctors he'd be lucky to live another five years—later he found out that they had actually given him less than a year. The door to the future (*any* future) had slammed shut, leaving him with the challenge of finding some way to support his family after he was gone: his wife and children, aged three, four and five.

One night very late in my hospital bed, I sat up and calculated that when I died in five years, I would have to have a million dollars to cover my children's future. This was an unimaginable sum to a man earning fifteen thousand dollars a year, but that's what I would need. The hospital discharged me just after the New Year—out I went back into the world, but with a terminal diagnosis. As time and I stumbled on, I learned an obvious lesson: You can't save a million dollars in five years—not on fifteen thousand a year; not in a hundred years. I had to do better. I started a moonlight business, After Hours Advertising. It doubled my income, but by then I had only four years to live. I'd still never save a million dollars in that short time.

Then I had a brainstorm. My wife received money-saving coupons for store products in the mail. Manufacturers sent out billions of these cents-off coupons every year by direct mail. I would distribute them in a new way, printing them on a single sheet and selling them as a supplement to the Sunday newspapers. It would save the advertisers millions of dollars in direct-mail costs, and maybe it would make a million dollars for me.

For two years I struggled with various ways to print and distribute coupons in newspapers, until finally my big break came. One sticky August afternoon the promotion manager of a major corporation called to ask, "Ted, is it reasonable for you to distribute thirty-five million coupons for us next January?" Up to then I'd never distributed a million anything.

I said, "No, it's not. But let me try." Thirty-five million coupons meant a $350,000 order for me, $250,000 in my pocket if I succeeded; a million-dollar bankruptcy if I didn't. I had to do it, and I did. Three months later I called them back to say, "I'm ready to go." Ninety days later I had $250,000 in the bank and I'd launched a new industry. Later that year, on December twenty-third, five years after my sleepless night in the hospital, I signed a contract to sell my new coupon business for over a million dollars—the money for my children's future.

By then I had discovered that even doctors can make mistakes. They had diagnosed my illness incorrectly, but for that I have to thank them. If it were not for receiving a diagnosis of terminal ill-

ness, I'd still be sitting behind a middle-management desk, pulling down a middle-management salary.

I did not die, nor do I expect to die soon. My desperation business is a billion-dollar industry. I enjoy the future I never expected to have in a house perched high above beautiful Kaneohe Bay, Hawaii.

I learned a lesson that long-ago night in the hospital: Don't wait for a death sentence to explode into action. Your future becomes what you make it.

Source: Arthur Pine with Julie Houston, *One Door Closes, Another Door Opens* (New York: Delacorte Press, 1993), 119–121.

6. *Hang loose. Take your dreams, your goals and your work seriously, but not yourself.* The principle purpose of life is to enjoy it, and taking yourself too seriously defeats the purpose. Furthermore, taking life too seriously will actually hurt your chances of reaching the winner's circle. When we take ourselves too seriously, we tend to physically and mentally tighten up. It hurts our creativity, and we tend to get very rigid in our behavior. That's the exact opposite of the kind of thinking and behavior needed to succeed in a rapidly changing world.

The most successful people in business aren't in it just for the money. If that were the case, most would have retired years ago. They enjoy playing the game of business much in the same way a golfer or tennis player enjoys playing the sport. Of course, they enjoy making money and aren't in business to lose it. But the money to them is just a way to keep score as they ply their skills in the marketplace. It's about learning, growing, being of service, helping others and having a good time.

It's been said that you grow up the day you learn how to laugh at yourself. So, as you pursue your dreams, learn to put unexpected setbacks in perspective. The present tends to make us nearsighted. Ask yourself, "How important will this be in twenty years?" You can be sure it won't matter at all in a hundred years. Hang loose, be flexible, treat it like a game, enjoy the journey and leave the long faces to those who are going to live forever.

7. *Never, never, never quit.* That's the key to long-term success. While you may have to take a lot of detours and encounter a lot of dirt roads along the way, the spirit of undying determination is what will ultimately carry you to the winner's circle.

It's common for major business successes to be preceded by numerous business failures. Before building Disneyland, Walt Disney went bankrupt several times. Research at the University of Georgia suggests that entrepreneurs get smarter with each succeeding bankruptcy. According to the data, ten business failures all but guarantee a successful eleventh attempt.

I've never been bankrupt, and I definitely don't recommend it. But the lesson is that persistence can make you rich. One home run makes all the strikeouts worthwhile. The winners are the ones who keep swinging. As the late author Og Mandino wrote, "So long as there's a breath in me, that long I will persist. For now I know one of the greatest principles of success; if I persist long enough I will win."

OWN THE MARKET INSTEAD OF TRYING TO BEAT THE MARKET

It usually takes a long time for investors to become sophisticated enough to realize how simple investing can be.

—PETER DI TERESA, SENIOR
ANALYST, MORNINGSTAR.COM

We all rely on experts to help us solve problems that we know
little or nothing about. When such a problem comes into our
life, we think:

- I don't have the time or expertise to handle this.
- There are knowledgeable, experienced professionals
  who know far more about this than I ever will.
- I need to find and pay someone who can take care of
  this for me.
- If it's an important problem, I need to find the best person I can. Good help isn't cheap, and cheap help usually
  isn't good. The people who charge top dollar are usually
  worth far more than they are paid.

That type of thinking usually leads you to the right physician, accountant, attorney, appliance-repair service, architect, engineer or anyone in almost any area of expertise. Time is the scarce resource. We need to focus our life energy on what we do best and delegate technical problems to experts.

Because relying on experts helps in so many areas of life, it's only natural to search for an expert who can help us invest our money. Unfortunately, this is one area where experts can do more harm than good. When it comes to picking future winning investments, there are no experts. Your time spent searching for an excellent stock picker might as well be spent searching for the tooth fairy. Anyone who tells you that he or she can consistently beat the market is either lying or self-delusional, because stock-market fluctuations are random and unpredictable. As an anonymous but very wise soul once said: "There are three kinds of investors:

1. Investors who don't know what the market will do—and know they don't know.

2. Investors who don't know what the market will do—but think they do know.

3. Investors who don't know what the market will do—and get paid a lot to pretend they know."

There is only one thing we do know about the stock market: The longer you hold a large number of well-diversified stocks, the likelier they are to earn you more money than any other type of investment. While short-term stock-market fluctuations are random, the only long-term trend is up. Stocks held over decades will make you rich.

GURUS UNLIMITED

Most of the entire investment industry and the accompanying media of books, magazines, newsletters, radio, television and websites want you to believe that experts know how to consistently beat the market. They want you to believe that myth because their livelihood depends on it. If the market is unpredictable, then stock pickers, gurus and pundits are irrelevant. You wouldn't need them. You would just buy index funds, keep your costs low, ignore the brokers, money managers, media gurus, investment-seminar hacks and you'd do fine. It turns out that's precisely what you should do.

Unfortunately, that's what most investors don't do. Instead, we cling to the belief that there are experts out there holding the Holy Grail to superior future returns. (I say "we" because for many years I believed this, too.) If we can only find the right person, his or her knowledge, instincts and superior brainpower will make us rich. Or maybe we can find someone to teach us the tricks to superior investing that worked for them. It's the triumph of wishful thinking over facts. Three well-known cases come to mind.

The first and perhaps most well-known case is the Beardstown Ladies. Fourteen grandmotherly women living in the vicinity of Beardstown, Illinois, created an investment club. Lo and behold, their investments delivered a ten-year average annual return of a whopping 23.4%, while the S&P 500 Index averaged a 14.9% return for the same period. What a story! Fourteen small-town midwestern grandmas beat the street and are eager to teach us how they did it in their new book.

It was a publicists' dream come true. The Beardstown Ladies' first book was a best-seller in 1994. It quickly turned into a media circus of more books, hundreds of speeches and a host of television appearances. The fairy tale ended in 1998 when someone decided to see if the claim of 23.4% average returns was actually correct. Unfortunately, the Beardstown Ladies' boast was less than accurate. As they say in the NFL, "after further review," their actual ten-year average returns turned out to be only 9.1%.

In retrospect, we all should have known better and checked their returns sooner. The idea of fourteen Illinois grandmothers beating the market by such a wide margin for ten years is about as far-fetched as the idea of them beating the Chicago Bears on a cold December day at Soldier Field.

Okay, so the Beardstown Ladies didn't beat the market. How about people with superior brainpower? Certainly they must have an edge when it comes to investing. It seems plausible until you learn about the performance of the Mensa Investment Club. Mensa is an organization whose membership is restricted to people who score in the top 2% on I.Q. tests. According to *Smart Money* magazine, over a fifteen-year period when the S&P 500 averaged an annual return of 15.3%, the Mensa Investment Club averaged a meager 2.5%. One club member saw his investment grow from $3,500 to $9,300 over a thirty-five-year span. During the same time, $3,500 invested in the S&P 500 grew to $291,076. If someone ever asks you, "Why aren't you rich?," you now have a perfect excuse. Tell them about the Mensa Investment Club and then say, "It's not my fault. I'm just too smart."

The fact that the Beardstown Ladies and Mensa Investment Club members lagged the market doesn't prove that there aren't knowledgeable, experienced professionals who can outperform it. While those first two cases are more entertaining than conclusive, the next one might give you serious reservations the next time you see an ad or hear a broker boasting about market-beating abilities.

Imagine being able to assemble an investment dream team with members possessing incredible intellect, coupled with extreme knowledge of world stock markets and Nobel Prize–winning credentials. Such a team was assembled in 1994 at a company called Long-Term Capital Management (LTCM). Convinced they had created a method to eliminate risk from investing, LTCM launched a giant hedge fund promising that through the use of mathematical models, they would make investors enormous sums of money. The minimum investment allowed was $10 million, and the money couldn't be withdrawn for three years. The enormous reputation of the dream team had wealthy investors clamoring to get in on the action. In a few months LTCM raised over $3 billion and began investing worldwide.

At first the company had incredible success, posting returns of 20%, 43% and 41% in the first three years. Markets behaved in accordance with the formulas' predictions. But in 1997 the markets stopped acting so predictably. A financial panic swept across Asia, banks failed and prices plummeted. Instead of getting out, LTCM held positions because the model said that eventually everything would return to normal. Soon LTCM began to hemorrhage money, and debts exceeded $100 billion. The company faced bankruptcy, but if it failed, it would take with it the value of positions it held around the globe, totaling $1.25 trillion—an amount equal to the annual budget of the U.S. government.

To prevent a global economic collapse, the Federal Reserve organized a bailout of LTCM, with fourteen banks putting up $3.6 billion to buy out the fund. The dream team and their investors lost millions. In December 1999, LTCM fully repaid the banks that prevented its collapse. Shortly thereafter, the fund was closed.

You can read more about the story of Long-Term Capital Management in Roger Lowenstein's book *When Genius Failed;* and *Trillion Dollar Bet* is an excellent PBS NOVA documentary on the subject, available on video. The lesson is that genius and mathematical sophistication have no edge when it comes to predicting future market behavior. In *Trillion Dollar Bet,* Nobel Prize–winning economist Paul Samuelson (not a member of the dream team) says, "There is a tempting and fatal fascination in mathematics. Albert Einstein warned against it. He said elegance is for tailors. Don't believe in something because it's a beautiful formula. There will always be room for judgment."

The Beardstown Ladies, the Mensa Investment Club and Long-Term Capital Management all illustrate what legendary baseball manager Casey Stengel told us many years ago: "Forecasting is very difficult, especially if it involves the future."

WHY PASSIVE INVESTING WORKS

I'm sure you've heard the old saying "If it sounds too good to be true, it probably is," especially when it comes to matters of money. But it turns out that simple buy-and-hold index investing is one of the best, most efficient ways to grow your money to the ultimate goal of financial freedom. Better yet, it comes with an enormous time bonus. You don't have to spend countless hours learning about the complexities of investing. You don't have to spend more hours agonizing over what investments to buy or sell, or when to buy and sell them, which means more freedom for you while your money compounds on autopilot.

Here, in a nutshell, are seven reasons why no-load index investing is so effective:

1. *No sales commissions.* If you buy a load fund from a broker, you usually pay a 4% to 6% sales commission that goes straight into the broker's pocket. That's money you'll never see again. With a no-load index fund, 100% of your initial investment, minus very low transaction costs, goes to work for you. Don't let a broker tell you that load funds perform better. It simply isn't true.

2. *Low yearly expenses.* The typical mutual fund has an annual expense ratio of 1 to 2%. That means that between 1 and 2% is deducted from the balance of your fund account every year to cover the expenses of running the fund. On the other hand, a low-cost index fund's yearly expenses can run as little as .18% per year, and most are well under .5% per year. That may not seem like much, but small annual expenses become very costly when compounded over time. For example, consider an investor who puts $10,000 in a mutual fund with an annual return of 10% before expenses and leaves it there for 20 years. With an annual expense ratio of 1.5%, the amount would grow to $49,725. But with an expense ratio of .5%, the amount would grow to $60,858, or 18% more. In his farewell speech as chairman of the Securities and Exchange Commission, Arthur Levitt, Jr., remarked, "Without paying attention to costs, an investor stands a better chance of earning a million dollars as a contestant on *Survivor*."

3. *Diversity*. If you own only one stock and the company goes out of business, you lose all of your investment. The more companies you own, the lower the odds are of that happening. By owning an entire market of funds, you have the ultimate in diversity, a crucial factor in safe investing.

4. *Indexing takes the emotional component out of investing.* Two emotions that can ruin any investor are greed and fear. They cause us to buy high and sell low instead of vice versa. Ego and overconfidence ruin portfolios, too. We think we know what's going to be hot and what's not. We think we can time the market or that we can hire an expert who can. It's possible but very unlikely. Trying to beat the market over time is trying to win at what noted Wall Street authority Charles Ellis calls "the loser's game." *You have to know what you don't know.* In a study examining over sixty-six thousand discount-brokerage accounts over a six-year period, University of California at Davis finance professors Brad Barber and Terry Odean found that those who did the least trading earned returns that were an average of 62% higher than those who did the most. Barber and Odean also found that women investors outearned men investors by an average of 1.4% per year because they traded less. When we pick an asset allocation, buy the market and hold it, we invest with a sound plan independent of our emotional impulses.

5. *Index funds are very tax-efficient.* Because you hold an entire market of funds, there is very little turnover in the portfolio to trigger a large and unexpected capital-gains tax bill.

6. *You don't have to worry about the competency of the fund manager.* Good mutual-fund managers are like winning coaches. When they get a good track record, another company hires them away for more money to manage another fund. The next manager of a fund you own could be the village idiot who ends up costing you dearly. It's happened more than once. Index funds are not dependent on the stock-picking skills of a manager.

7. *You don't have to pay a money manager to monitor your investments.* A typical money manager charges from 1 to 3% of the balance of your portfolio every year to manage your account. That takes another large bite out of your returns.

In short, *the main reason index investing is so successful is because fewer people have their hands in your pockets.* The typical managed fund has to outperform its equivalent index by 1 to 2% per year just to equal the index. That's very difficult for most funds to do over an extended period of time. Throw in the added bonuses of no sales charges, tax efficiency, no money-management fees, and it's easy to see why buy-and-hold index investing works so well. By being content to settle for slightly less than average returns, you end up with far above average returns compared to most investors. As Burton Malkiel wrote in *The Wall Street Journal,* "Over a 30-year period ending in 1998, a $10,000 investment in the S&P 500 Index would have grown to $311,000 (after expenses); in the average general equity fund, the same investment would have grown to $171,950."

There is one drawback to index funds. They're boring. You

don't get to chase the action. You don't get to go to the party and brag about your new tech stock that jumped 100% last month or your market-timing skills. You aren't going to experience the super highs of winning big and the super lows of great losses. The stock market has become the casino of choice for many people. And most of those people are paying the price by taking years longer, if ever, to reach financial freedom. If you are tempted to think that you or anyone else can time the market, consider this:

A study by Ibbotson Associates of Chicago found that over the 70 years from 1925 to 1995, an investment of $1 in the S&P 500 index grew to $1,114. But for an investor who missed the best 35 months of that 840-month period, $1 grew to only $10. In other words, 99% of the gains occurred during just 4% of the time.

Timing the market is for losers. Time *in* the market will get you to the winner's circle, and you'll sleep a lot better at night.

Overwhelming Support for Passive Investing

If you read the works of leading investment authors, scholars and practitioners, one fact stands out: The vast majority overwhelmingly recommend buying and holding no-load, low-cost index funds. Here are what some of them have to say on the subject of indexing:

Paul Samuelson, first American to win the Nobel Prize in economic science: "The most efficient way to diversify a stock portfolio is with a low-fee index fund. Statistically, a broadly based stock-index fund will outperform most actively managed equity portfolios."

Warren Buffet, chairman of Berkshire Hathaway and investor of legendary repute: "Most investors, both institutional and individual, will find that the best way to own common stocks is through an index fund that charges minimal fees. Those following this path are sure to beat the net results (after fees and expenses) delivered by the great majority of investment professionals."

Jane Bryant Quinn, financial columnist for *Newsweek* and author of *Making the Most of Your Money:* "Indexing is for winners only."

Burton Malkiel, professor of economics, Princeton University, and author of *A Random Walk Down Wall Street:* "Index funds allow investors an opportunity to buy securities of all different types, and are a sensible, serviceable method of obtaining the benefits of equity investing with no effort, minimal expense, and considerable tax savings."

Jason Zweig, senior writer and columnist, *Money* magazine: "If you buy—and then hold—a total-stock-market index fund, it is mathematically certain that you will outperform the vast majority of all other investors in the long run."

Andrew Tobias, author of *The Only Investment Guide You'll Ever Need:* "If the professionals do no better than darts—and most do not—then how much is it worth to have them manage your money?"

Charles Schwab, founder and chairman of the board, the Charles Schwab Corporation: "Only about one out of every four equity funds outperforms the stock market. That's why I'm a firm believer in the power of indexing."

Douglas R. Sease, author of *Winning with the Market* and former financial editor of *The Wall Street Journal:* "You will never see an S&P index fund leading the best-performance charts in *The Wall Street Journal.* But—and this is the point—your fund's returns will almost certainly beat those of the majority of actively managed funds over a period of five years or more. And you will never see an S&P index fund at the bottom of *The Wall Street Journal* performance charts, either."

John C. Bogle, founder and chairman emeritus, the Vanguard Group: "Of 355 stock funds in existence 30 years ago, 189 failed even to survive. And only 14—roughly 1 in 25—beat the return of the stock market as a whole by as much as a percentage point a year on average."

William Bernstein, Ph.D., M.D., author of *The Intelligent Asset Allocator* and frequent guest columnist for *Morningstar;* "Through hard experience, I've found that it's almost always a bad idea to fall in love with an active manager and abandon an indexed approach."

Jonathan Clements, author of the popular *Wall Street Journal* column "Getting Going": "As a group, investors in U.S. stocks can't outperform the market because, collectively, they are the market. In fact, once you figure in investment costs, active investors are destined to lag behind Wilshire 5000 index funds, because these active investors incur far higher investment costs."

Douglas Dial, portfolio manager of the CREF stock account fund of TIAA-CREF: "Indexing is a marvelous technique. I wasn't a true believer. I was just an ignoramus. Now I am a convert. Indexing is an extraordinarily sophisticated thing to do."

Rex Sinquefield, co-chairman of Dimensional Fund Advisors: "The only consistent superior performer is the market itself, and the only way to capture that superior consistency is to invest in a properly diversified portfolio of index funds."

Eric Tyson, author of *Investing for Dummies* and *Mutual Funds for Dummies:* "Why waste your time trying to select and manage a portfolio of individual stocks when you can replicate the market average returns (and beat the majority of professional money managers) through an exceptionally underrated and underused investment fund called an index fund.

William F. Sharpe, Nobel laureate and chairman, Financial Engines, Inc.: "I love index funds."

Larry E. Swedroe, author of *What Wall Street Doesn't Want You to Know:* "Despite the superior returns generated by passively managed funds, financial publications are dominated by forecasts from so-called gurus and the latest hot fund managers. I believe that there is a simple explanation for the misinformation: It's just not in the interests of the Wall Street establishment or the financial press to inform investors of the failure of active managers."

Jeremy J. Siegel, professor of finance, Wharton School, University of Pennsylvania, and author of *Stocks for the Long Run:* "There is a crucially important difference about playing the game of investing compared to virtually any other activity. Most of us have no chance of being as good as the *average* in any pursuit where others practice and hone skills for many, many hours. But we can be as good as the average investor in the stock market with no practice at all."

The next time a broker, financial planner or money manager tells you that he can deliver market-beating returns, show him these quotes and then ask him, "What do you know that these leading authorities in the field don't know?"

HOW TO GET STARTED

As I pointed out in Insight 2, passive investing is sheer simplicity. Let's look at the steps in more detail to get you started.

1. *Decide on an asset allocation of stocks, bonds and cash.* This decision will be the single greatest determinant of how your portfolio performs over the long haul. Some years ago, Gary Brinson, a noted finance academic, studied a group of pension-fund managers and determined that over 90% of the difference in their performance was determined by how much each allocated among stocks, bonds and cash. The same will be true of your portfolio.

You should allocate somewhere between 50 and 80% of your money in stocks, depending on your age and risk tolerance. The younger you are, the higher the stock allocation should be. Any money you may need to spend in the next five years should definitely *not* be in stocks. Conversely, any money you aren't going to spend in the next ten years should be in stocks. As a popular saying goes, "Stocks make you rich, bonds keep you rich." A good starting point to determine the percentage you should allocate to stocks is to subtract your age from 120.

Assessing your risk tolerance is very important. During bull markets, when stock prices increase, nobody wants to own bonds. But during bear markets, when stock prices plummet, almost everyone wants more in bonds. You need enough money in bonds and cash so that when stock prices take a dive, as they inevitably will, you don't panic and sell. If you have financial staying power, patience and discipline, the market will eventually recover, surge to new highs and make you richer than ever. It's only a paper loss unless you sell. Only two prices matter with respect to investments: how much you pay when you buy, and how much you get when you sell. The rest is just noise.

My favorite way to assess risk tolerance is the 50% Rule. Ask yourself, "How would I feel if stock prices dropped 50%?" and adjust your allocation accordingly. For example, if you have 80% in stocks and stock prices drop 50%, the current value of your portfolio will decrease 40%. Would that keep you awake at night or cause you a lot of worry? Would you panic and sell your stock funds? If the answer to either question is yes, you need to have less money in stocks. Over the long term, stocks build wealth, but the short term is like riding a roller coaster. The wilder the ride, the greater the odds are of higher returns. Just be sure to choose a ride you can live with.

2. *Pick a reputable investment company that sells no-load, low-cost index funds.* I recommend doing business with one firm in order to keep things simple. Vanguard is an excellent company whose founder, John Bogle, pioneered index funds; they offer the greatest variety of index funds at the lowest cost. Other excellent companies are Fidelity, T. Rowe Price, Charles Schwab, USAA and TIAA-CREF. While plenty of companies offer index funds, not all index funds are created equal. Look for a company that charges no loads up front or on redemption and whose index funds have total annual expenses of less than .5%. Be careful and read the fine print. There's a lot of treachery out there in the form of hidden loads and fees. Costs matter.

3. *You don't need many funds.* In some cases, your portfolio can be as simple as one balanced index fund. A balanced index fund is a combination of stock and bond index funds. For example, with Vanguard's LifeStrategy balanced funds, you can choose an allocation of 25, 40, 60 or 80% stocks, with the rest in bonds and cash. For a young person starting an IRA, Vanguard's LifeStrategy Growth fund is a simple way to invest with an 80% stock allocation.

If you want more control over your allocation of stocks to bonds, your portfolio can include two funds. Choose a total stock-market index fund that mirrors the Wilshire 5000 Index and a bond index fund. The Wilshire 5000 is an index of the five thousand largest U.S. stocks and the closest representation of the total U.S. stock market.

For the bond portion of your portfolio, a total bond-market index fund that tracks the Lehman Brothers Aggregate Bond Index will fit the bill. If inflation concerns you, you might opt for one of the Treasury inflation-protection securities (also known as TIPS) funds. TIPS funds guarantee that your investment in bonds won't be eroded by inflation. Stay away from long-term and junk-bond funds. You want bonds in your portfolio to alleviate risk, and these kinds of bonds are too risky.

A two-index-fund portfolio doesn't give you any exposure to international stocks, but a strong case can be made that you don't need it. A huge percentage of the revenue from the largest U.S. companies comes from abroad. By owning a total stock-market index fund, you already have a good deal of international exposure.

Finally, you can have a four-fund portfolio consisting of a total stock-market index, a total international-stock index, a bond index and a money-market fund. How much you put in international stocks is up to you, but I keep my stock portfolio between 10 and 20% in international funds. Choose a total international fund that tracks the Morgan Stanley Capital International Europe, Australia, Far East Index (commonly referred to as the MSCI EAFE).

Keep your bond fund in your tax-deferred accounts, such as

an IRA, SEP, Keogh or 401(k), so the income they produce won't trigger yearly income taxes. If this isn't possible, consider using a tax-free municipal bond fund. Your CPA can advise you on this.

4. *Keep loading the wagon.* Saving and investing over time is what carries you to the winner's circle. Put a nice chunk of every paycheck into the portfolio according to your allocation. Saving is the hard part. The rest is easy.

5. *Check the portfolio once a year to see if it needs rebalancing.* If the allocation of stocks is within 10% of the targeted allocation, do nothing. If it needs rebalancing, do it by adding new monies or move money in tax-deferred accounts to prevent a tax bill.

6. *If you enjoy trying to beat the market, have your cake and eat it, too.* Allocate 5% of your portfolio to a "casino account" that lets you buy and sell without jeopardizing your future financial freedom. The odds are that you'll beat the index about 20 to 30% of the time. Have fun and enjoy your winnings, but don't make the mistake of thinking you're smarter than the market and start trading with the rest of your portfolio. As a popular Wall Street saying goes, "Bulls make money, bears make money and hogs get slaughtered."

7. *Ignore people who tell you that the era of indexing is over.* If you believe that, you believe the era of discount pricing is over. There will be years when most actively managed funds outperform the index. In years when the stock market is down, most actively managed funds beat the index, because actively managed funds keep about 5% of their money in cash, while index funds are totally invested. Every year some actively managed funds will outperform the market. The problem is that predicting which ones will do it in advance is very difficult, if not impossible.

My friend Taylor Larimore, correctly labeled by *Money* magazine as "Dean of the Vanguard Diehards," summarized the index advantage best: "Index funds offer much more than superior returns. They also provide maximum diversification, no overlap, no style drift, no manager changes, lower turnover, lower expenses, lower taxes, greater simplicity and peace of mind." Own the market. You'll be glad you did.

Investment Advice in Very Few Words

Some time back I ran across an item written by Less Antman, a Bonsall, California, CPA who also runs an excellent message board at www.simplyrich.com. Here, courtesy of Less, is:

The Best Investment Advice in Under Ten Words

1. The best tax shelter in America today . . . buy-and-hold.
2. The surest way to outperform 80% of all stock-market investors over the long term . . . index.
3. The surest way to outperform the indexes over the long term . . . miscalculate. (Witness the Beardstown Ladies.)
4. Where to start if you have at least $3,000 to invest . . . Vanguard. (You can open an IRA with $1,000.)
5. Where to start if you have only $25 to invest . . . TIAA-CREF.
6. The surest way to guarantee you don't outlive your retirement savings . . . smoke.
7. The cause that deserves a contribution from you every year . . . Roth.
8. The people who benefit most from variable annuities . . . salesmen.
9. The quickest way to reduce your tax bill . . . day-trade.

In keeping with the spirit of less is more, here is a summary of key points we have covered about money thus far:

The Most Important Wealth-Building Words

The six most important wealth-building words are:
Make your money work for you.

The five most important wealth-building words are:
Have an asset-allocation plan.

The four most important wealth-building words are:
Keep your costs low.

The three most important wealth-building words are:
Own the market.

The two most important wealth-building words are:
Compound interest.

And the most important wealth-building word is:
Save.

Commit those words to memory, repeat them to yourself once a day, follow the advice and they will serve you well.

LIMIT YOUR LOSSES INSTEAD OF LETTING BAD LUCK RUIN YOU

The time to fix the roof is when the sun is shining.

—ANONYMOUS

Life is not fair, and we all get our share of bad breaks. Worse yet, most bad breaks happen without warning. That's unavoidable.

What you can avoid is allowing misfortune to ruin you financially. That's what this choice is about—damage control. In short, you take care of the bad stuff up front by carrying the proper types and amounts of insurance. You look at the future and ask yourself, "What if someone in my family and/or I:

- Encounter a lengthy, expensive illness?
- Are disabled and can't work?
- Lose or have major damage done to our home?
- Become the defendant in an expensive lawsuit?
- Die?
- Are involved in a major automobile accident?
- Need long-term care?"

As I mentioned earlier, winners become and stay financially free by being good risk managers. And one key to good risk management is to cover the downside. It takes only one major misfortune to foreclose your chances of reaching the winner's circle. Being properly insured is a must.

Admittedly, insurance is not the most scintillating or exciting of subjects. One title you'll never see at your local bookstore is *The Joy of Insurance*. Nevertheless, it's crucial to know what types and amounts of coverage you need. It's another key ingredient to creating the millionaire in you.

The overriding principles for being properly insured are simple:

1. Insure against only the big calamities that you can't afford to pay out of pocket.
2. Take the largest deductible you can afford in the event of a misfortune.
3. Buy coverage only from the best-rated insurance companies.

THREE TYPES OF INSURANCE MISTAKES

It's estimated that 90% of us don't carry the proper types and amount of insurance. Let's face it: Planning for potential disasters and listening to insurance sales pitches are about as enjoyable as a migraine. Since we don't like to think about such topics, we tend to avoid them. As a result, common and potentially costly mistakes are made when buying insurance.

One mistake is insuring relatively unimportant areas and not insuring critical ones. You don't have to look very far to find people who carry extended-service warranties on their cars or big-screen TVs but fail to carry sufficient health care. Lots of people insure packages at the post office but leave themselves vulnerable to an expensive lawsuit. And it's common to find single people without dependents carrying needless, expensive life-insurance policies while the long-term disability coverage that they really need goes begging.

Another common mistake is deciding whether or not to purchase a particular type of insurance based on the odds of something happening. For example, if floods or earthquakes rarely occur where you live, you may think that it's a waste of money to add that kind of coverage to your homeowner's policy. Not so. The odds of something happening don't matter. The only thing that matters is this: If a freak earthquake or flood destroyed your home, would you be financially devastated? If the answer is yes, then be sure your insurance covers it. If the odds of it happening are small, the additional cost will be cheap, and it's coverage you can't afford to be without. Don't buy insurance based on the odds of something happening. Buy insurance to protect yourself and others from what you can't afford to have happen.

A third common type of mistake is insuring too narrowly. For example, you can buy flight insurance that will pay a beneficiary of your choice if you die in a commercial-airline crash. It's very cheap. It's also a waste of money. You either need life insurance or you don't. If you need it, you need a comprehensive policy that pays off in the event of your death no matter the cause. Similarly, people often buy health-care policies to insure against specific diseases such as cancer or Alzheimer's disease. What you need is a comprehensive major-medical policy that protects you from enormous health-care costs no matter what accident or illness befalls you.

To be alive is to be vulnerable to misfortune. But the odds are overwhelming that you won't know in advance what specific kinds of bad breaks will strike you or when. As you decide on what types and amounts of insurance you need, let this motto be your guide: *"It's the bus you don't see that hits you."* Prepare for the unexpected. Let's look at some common types of insurance you need to consider.

LIFE INSURANCE

The only valid reason to buy life insurance is to provide income to dependents who would be financially deprived in the event of your death. If you are financially independent or have no dependents, you don't need it. If you need it, buy inexpensive term insurance and ignore all the sales pitches for cash-value policies such as whole life, universal life and variable universal life. Cash-value policies are investment vehicles, but too many people have their hands in your pockets to make them a good deal. That worn-out phrase about life insurance being a good investment is true for the company and the person selling the policy. Insurance salespeople push cash-value policies because that's where the money is—for them. It's typical for 50 to 100% of the first year's premium to go straight into the salesperson's pocket. Insurance is for protection, and investments are for growing your nest egg. Don't mix the two.

If you are young and have no dependents, don't let a sales-person talk you into buying life insurance because you can get it cheap while you are young and still insurable. Your money is better invested in an index fund. Don't buy life insurance unless and until you need it.

If you need life insurance, a good rule of thumb is to carry between five and eight times your yearly after-tax income. For example, if you earn $50,000 per year after taxes, you should carry a policy with a face value of between $250,000 and $400,000. If you are a two-income family that depends heavily on both incomes, both of you should be insured.

When you purchase term insurance, you lock in the rate you pay for a specific period such as five, ten, fifteen or twenty years. The longer the period during which your rates can't be raised, the higher the annual premium will be. Buy the longest guaranteed period that you need and can afford. Be sure the policy is guaranteed renewable, meaning that they can't deny you coverage in the future due to poor health. Good policies will have that feature.

Once you reach the winner's circle, you can probably drop the policy, unless you have a large estate. Life insurance can be a good investment to pay estate taxes when you are leaving money to heirs other than your spouse; see an independent financial planner or an estate-planning attorney for guidance. But for most people, life insurance is death insurance. Die as cheaply as you can.

DON'T OVERLOOK LONG-TERM DISABILITY

Hear me loud and clear: *If you aren't financially independent, you need long-term disability coverage*. While 70% of Americans carry life insurance, only 40% carry any form of disability insurance. Yet the odds are one in five that a thirty-five-year-old person will become disabled before age sixty-five, and one in seven will be disabled for at least five years.

How crucial is long-term disability coverage? Consider this: If you die, your living expenses are over. If you're disabled, you still have to eat and put a roof over your head. At the same time, you're hit with the double misfortunes of not being able to earn an income alongside potentially huge health-care costs.

Buy as much disability coverage as you can afford. The maximum amount you can purchase usually replaces 60% of your income. Don't rely on your employer's policy. Buy your own policy with your own after-tax dollars; if you ever need to collect, the benefits will be tax-free. And in today's free-agent economy, you don't want to be dependent on your employer for disability coverage. Other features of a good disability policy:

- It is noncancelable and guaranteed renewable to age sixty-five.
- It covers your inability to work at your own occupation.

- It provides the longest benefit in your own occupation for as long as possible or at least until age sixty-five.
- It has a cost-of-living adjustment.
- It provides benefits for partial disability.
- It has a waiting period of no more than ninety days before coverage begins.

According to Northwestern Mutual Life Insurance Company, one year of total disability can erase ten years of savings for someone who saves 10% of their income annually. When you consider that someone in their forties is far more likely to become disabled than to die, this is one kind of insurance that future millionaires need. Long-term disability coverage insures your future earnings. If you aren't financially independent, your future earnings are your most valuable financial asset.

HEALTH CARE

Consider yourself among the fortunate if you have health insurance through your employer or a group plan. It's usually far less expensive. Believe it or not, an estimated forty-four million Americans have no health-care coverage.

Some years ago I knew a Ph.D. psychologist who is a very bright, talented, successful and responsible person. When he was in his midfifties, he unexpectedly suffered a major heart attack requiring open-heart surgery. Much to my surprise, I learned that he carried no health insurance and had to pay a $70,000 hospital bill out of his own pocket. That was in the early nineties. I shudder to think what the bill would be today. Had I been him, just seeing the bill would have made more than my coronary arteries go into spasm.

If you have to shop for a health plan, look for major medical coverage that pays the big bills such as hospitalization, X rays, lab work, surgery, doctors' charges and rehabilitation services. Make sure the policy's lifetime maximum benefit is at least $1 million. You can keep the cost down by taking the largest deductible and copayment percentage that you can afford. Copayment is the dollar amount the policy requires that you pay before coverage begins, such as $25 for doctor visits, $20 for prescription bills or 20% of your hospital bill. Copayment percentages are usually capped at something like $1,000, meaning if you have a large bill you would pay only $200 out of pocket, with a 20% copayment and a $1,000 maximum out-of-pocket expense per year.

Joining an HMO (health maintenance organization) will lower your premiums but restrict your choice of physicians and some services. As with most things in life, with health-care insurance you get what you pay for. So if the freedom to select your own physician is important to you, it's best to steer away from an HMO.

In addition to a high maximum lifetime benefit, here are several features of an excellent health plan:

- The freedom to see the doctor of your choice, or specialists without referral or the need to obtain authorization from a primary-care physician.
- No dollar limits on expenses such as hospital-room rates, surgeries, procedures and lab work.
- An annual limit or cap on the amount of money you have to pay out of pocket.
- International coverage, so if you are out of the country and need to obtain health care, it will be covered by your policy.

That's the ideal, and you may not want or be able to afford all of those features. You're likely to find a health-care plan that's right for you by shopping at the larger and more established companies.

COVER YOUR ASSETS

Thus far we have looked at insurance that focuses on protecting you and your loved ones in the event of death, disability or illness. Now let's look at insurance aimed at protecting what you already own.

First, you need a homeowner's or renter's policy to cover your residence and its contents in the event of a fire, flood, earthquake, robbery or any major catastrophe. The operative words in buying this type of coverage are *replacement cost*. For example, maybe you purchased your home years ago for $100,000, but it would cost twice that amount to rebuild if it were destroyed. Insure your home and its contents based on the amount it would cost you to replace the assets.

Don't assume that your policy covers all disasters such as floods and earthquakes, because it probably doesn't. You usually have to purchase a rider. Do it. Cover all potential disasters.

Make a list of all personal possessions in your home or apartment and store the list in a safe-deposit box or somewhere off the premises. An even better and quicker way to document your possessions is to go through the house with a video camera and record everything you own. Update the video once a year and store it somewhere other than your domicile. It will be extremely useful if you ever have to make a claim.

A homeowner's policy will generally insure personal property inside the home in an amount of 50 to 75% of the building's coverage, and this is usually sufficient. You will probably have to purchase a special rider to cover certain items such as expensive jewelry, computers, silverware or furs. Unless losing such items would constitute a financial catastrophe for you, it probably isn't worth buying.

Next to a home, the most expensive asset most people own is a car. While the law requires every licensed driver to carry bodily injury/property-damage liability coverage, most auto policies cover a lot more. Some features are necessary, and some are a waste of money if you have other policies or an older car. For example, if you drive an old car with a low blue-book value, consider dropping the comprehensive and collision coverage. Once again, the only good purpose for carrying insurance is to protect yourself from the catastrophes you can't afford. Other add-ons such as rental-car reimbursement and towing hardly qualify as disaster prevention and can be skipped. If you have a good health-care plan, you can also skip coverage for medical payments.

You can reduce the cost of homeowner's, renter's and auto insurance by taking the largest possible deductible you can afford. You'll probably be entitled to a discount if your home has a security system or fire sprinklers. Auto-insurance discounts are often given if your car has a security system, antilock brakes or air bags. Be sure to tell your agent if your car has them.

If you own a business, make sure your business policy covers contingencies. With home-based businesses on the rise, a fire can destroy a home and a business simultaneously. You need an additional business policy to cover the loss of inventories, computers and office equipment. If you own a home-based business and want to protect its assets, ask your insurance agent about a business policy.

Last but definitely not least, *insure yourself against potential lawsuits*. Purchase a personal liability umbrella policy of $1 million more than your net worth. Umbrella policies are relatively cheap for the amount of protection and are usually sold in $1 million increments. In our litigious society, it's an absolute must.

LONG-TERM CARE INSURANCE

Sue Stevens, director of financial planning for Morningstar Associates, makes this compelling case for carrying long-term care coverage:

Five out of a thousand people will experience a house fire: average cost, $3,400. Seventy out of a thousand people will have an auto accident: average cost, $3,000. Six hundred out of a thousand people will require a nursing-home stay: average cost, $50,000 per year with an average stay of three to five years.

Please don't misunderstand me. If you're under fifty, you don't need to rush out and buy long-term care insurance. In fact, two groups of people will never need it—those with very high net worth and those with little or no net worth. If you have little or no savings, you'll qualify for Medicaid, which means the government will pay for your nursing-home care. Medicaid is the nursing-home equivalent of welfare, which means you won't likely get the best of care, but you won't be paying for it, either. On the other hand, if you have several million dollars put away in liquid investments, you'll probably be able to pay for long-term care out of your own pocket.

However, if you find yourself with a net worth of between $200,000 and $3 million when you reach your fifties, give serious consideration to buying long-term care policies for you and your spouse. With continuing advancements in health and medical care, more people are going to be living longer. Add to the mix the seventy-eight million baby boomers who will be retiring over the next several decades, and it's a sure bet that many more people are going to require nursing-home, assisted-living or home-health care for extended periods of time.

My wife, Elke, and I both have long-term care policies, although I doubt we will ever need them. We purchased them in our fifties while the rates were relatively low and we were insurable and in good health. I think of our long-term care policies as a version of long-term disability insurance. If one of us requires long-term care for an extended period of time, it won't consume the investments that provide our retirement income.

If you go shopping for a long-term care policy, here are some of the features a good one will contain:

- A daily benefit equal to the current daily cost of a nursing home in the area where you live. The higher the benefit, the higher your premium will be.
- Inflation protection of 5% per year compounded to keep your daily benefit current with rising costs of care.
- A benefit payment period of at least three to five years. A lifetime benefit payment period is best.
- An elimination period you can afford. The elimination period is like a deductible. The longer you can pay out of pocket before the benefits kick in, the cheaper your premium will be. Medicare will pay for about the first twenty-five days. One hundred days is a good elimination period for most people.
- Coverage cannot be canceled for any reason other than for failure to pay premiums.
- The policy should cover both skilled and nonskilled care. Benefits should also cover home-health and assisted-living care without requiring a prior hospital stay.
- There are no exclusions for particular illnesses such as Alzheimer's disease and dementia.
- Benefit triggers that specify when coverage begins. The inability to dress or bathe are examples of benefit triggers. In the best and most expensive policies, proof of cognitive impairment such as Alzheimer's is a benefit trigger even if the person is able to dress and bathe.
- Waiver of premium, which allows you to stop making payments when coverage begins.
- Your annual premium cannot be raised unless it's raised for every policy holder living in your state.
- The policy is tax-qualified. With a qualified policy, the premium may be tax-deductible, and any benefits you receive will not be subject to federal taxes.

It's a good idea to purchase long-term care before age sixty. If you wait until age seventy, your premiums will be about two and a half times higher than at age sixty. Furthermore, the longer you wait, the greater your risk of contracting a chronic illness, which will make you uninsurable.

SHOPPING FOR COMPANIES, PRICES AND AGENTS

The Internet is making profound changes in the insurance industry by putting an enormous amount of information on the customer's desk. You can get an entire education on insurance by just reading the information posted on insurance websites. With the click of a mouse, you can get quotes and compare benefits. You can also check the financial strength and quality rating of an insurance company.

Here are some of the better insurance websites where you can learn more and/or shop for quotes:

- www.answerfinancial.com
- www.insure.com
- www.insurance.com
- www.insweb.com
- www.pivot.com
- www.quickquote.com
- www.quotesmith.com
- www.reliaquote.com

To check the financial strength and overall quality rating of an insurance company, go to www.ambest.com/ratings/search .html. The A. M. Best Company rates insurance companies from "A++" on down and has been doing it for over a century. *Only buy insurance from a company with an A. M. Best rating of "A" or better.*

What I have covered in this chapter is just a broad overview

of the types of insurance you may need. This information is by
no means all-inclusive, nor does it universally apply to everyone.
Find a good insurance agent to help determine what types of
coverage you need. A competent, customer-oriented agent will
save you both time and money. As you probably know, all insurance agents aren't created equal. Certain companies rigorously
screen and train their agents to provide the kind of service that
creates customer loyalty. Other companies hire whoever comes
in off the street and have extremely high turnover. Clearly you
want an agent with a track record of high ethics, professionalism and good service.

Start your search by asking for recommendations from
accountants, financial planners, lawyers and successful businesspeople whose judgment you trust. If several people recommend the same agent, that's an excellent sign.

You can also screen professional credentials such as:

- Chartered property casualty underwriter (CPCU)
- Certified life underwriter (CLU)
- Certified insurance counselor (CIC)

These and other designations indicate that the person has
spent time and energy studying to pass rigorous examinations
in their respective field. It demonstrates a serious commitment
to professionalism. You can search for a CPCU in your area
online at www.cpcusociety.org/consumer/agentbroker.shtml.
The CIC Society, at 800-632-2165, will send, on request, a list of
CIC agents who share your zip code.

Some agents represent only one company. Other agents are
independent, which gives them more latitude to shop for policies that make the most sense for you. Once you locate a good
agent, it's a good idea to give them as much of your insurance
business as you can. That way you become a more important
customer, and it's in that agent's best interest to see that you are

well covered and well served. A good agent will find you the policy that best fits your needs, not just the cheapest price. They won't sell you what you don't need and will stay in touch with you to see that your coverage is up to date and sufficient.

Finally, remember that the best and cheapest insurance is prevention:

- Don't smoke.
- Exercise regularly.
- If you drink, limit yourself to two drinks a day.
- Wear seat belts and don't drive under the influence.
- Eat the right foods and maintain your proper weight.
- Get enough rest.
- Get regular medical, dental and vision checkups.
- Smile and laugh a lot.

Yeah, bad stuff happens, but it's still a beautiful world.

LISTEN TO THOSE WHO KNOW INSTEAD OF THOSE WHO SELL

Your broker could be on his way to Hawaii right now because you bought the product of the month.

—ARTHUR LEVITT, JR., FORMER
CHAIRMAN, SECURITIES AND
EXCHANGE COMMISSION

I love Jewish humor. This is one of my favorite stories:

> Goldberg goes into Rubenstein's Deli and asks the owner, "Why are you so smart about money?"
>
> Rubenstein pauses, thinks for a moment and says, "I eat a lot of herring." For the next several weeks, Goldberg goes to the deli every day and eats copious amounts of herring.
>
> Then one day he walks into the deli looking very angry and tells Rubenstein, "The nerve of you, overcharging me for herring! Goldstein's Deli sells the same portion for half your price."
>
> Rubenstein smiles and says, "See? You're getting smarter already!"

Heaven knows, there's no shortage of information on how to be smart with your money. Every day we are bombarded with offers promising us great business and investment opportunities. Unfortunately, most of it comes with a hidden agenda that's costly at best and downright fraudulent at worst.

How do you separate the good information from the bad? That's what this choice is all about. You reach the winner's circle by:

- Listening to a few good sources and tuning out the rest
- Saying yes to a few good money-making opportunities and no to the rest.
- Knowing what kind of legal and financial advice you really need.
- Getting the advice and help you need at a reasonable price.

The first and most important key to getting the right advice at the right price is simple: *Get your advice and your investments from different sources.*

In other words, don't ask the barber if you need a haircut. The people who hit you over the head every day with great business and investment "opportunities" are salespeople who are far more interested in their wealth than yours.

There's nothing wrong with selling. We all make a living by selling something. But more often than not, in financial matters a conflict of interest exists between the buyer and the seller. Too often the salesperson's incentive is to sell you what's best for him or her rather than what's best for you. That's why it's imperative that your advisers be people who have no financial interest whatsoever in any business opportunity or investment you are considering. To do otherwise is naive at best and can be disastrous at worst. You need objective, unbiased third-party information and advice.

MASTERS OF THE WALLETECTOMY

People who long to separate you from your hard-earned money come in several varieties. Here are some of the more common types you are likely to encounter outside of the mainstream financial establishment.

Let's begin with illegal con artists. Although sometimes subtle, they are usually about as hard to spot as a bus because they promise fast, easy money with little or no effort on your part. For example, the Internal Revenue Service reports that thousands of African-Americans are being duped into paying between $30 and $200 to con artists who promise to file a "slave reparations" tax credit on their behalf. Of course, no such tax credit exists; the scam artists are just pocketing the fees they charge.

Similarly, if you have an e-mail address, you're likely to be bombarded with junk messages (commonly referred to as "spam") promising instant and incredible wealth. It's usually pitched as a wonderful business opportunity that's being offered to a select few, highly intelligent people like you. They claim to have made enormous sums of money in just a few months working part-time, and you can, too. Because there will always be people who are easily and willingly seduced by the promise of easy money, there will always be con artists trolling for business.

Then there are seminar and TV infomercial gurus who say they really want you to be rich. They promise to teach you the secrets to wealth if you'll just attend their courses and/or buy their products. The courses typically cover such topics as buying real estate with no money down; commodities trading; day trading; options trading; or any number of so-called secrets to wealth. In truth, they couldn't care less if you get rich. Their true agenda is for you to make them rich by buying an endless supply of their books, tapes and seminars. It's common for seminar and infomercial gurus to go bankrupt, get sued and incur tax liens from the IRS, and some have been imprisoned for fraud. Does that sound like a credible source of financial advice to you?

A third group is multilevel-marketing (MLM, also known as network-marketing) companies who tell you that by joining their network you can go into business for yourself, work from home and become enormously wealthy. You have probably gotten at least one sales pitch from a well-meaning friend, relative or neighbor who recently signed up and believes they have found the sure path to riches. You are asked to join, buy a start-up kit for about $100 and recruit other distributors who, in turn, recruit more distributors and so on. Those people are called your "downline." You get a commission on all the products you sell and all the products sold by members of your downline.

Is it possible to get rich in network marketing? Yes, it is. It's also possible to get rich playing the lottery, but the odds are overwhelmingly against you. The same is true with MLM. As I pointed out in Choice 2, getting to the winner's circle almost always requires stacking the odds in your favor. In a nation where one in fourteen households has a net worth of over $1 million, the typical active MLM distributor makes just a few hundred dollars a month, and well over 90% earn less than poverty-level wages. Many of the big-money MLM distributors make much, if not most, of their income by holding motivational rallies and selling success books and tapes to their downline. Recruits are told that the books and tapes are optional, but so is success.

To be sure, there are legitimate network marketing companies who will tell you the truth about earnings if you ask them. Some even post average earnings on their websites.

Joining a network-marketing company because you like the people, the products, the rallies, the books, the tapes and all that goes with it are all valid reasons if you can afford to do it. Much of what you learn in MLM about personal selling, goal setting, motivation and success are valuable lessons that can benefit you in other careers and areas of your life. But if your goal is to get to the winner's circle, the odds are much better elsewhere. Invest your time and money in getting a good education. Start a business of your own instead of buying a business in a box. Choose a career in something you feel passionate about instead of one being sold to you. And put the money you were going to invest in MLM into no-load, low-cost index funds instead. For most who try it, MLM means "many losing money" and an enormous waste of time.

Walletectomy-Artist-Detection Checklist

Regardless of the vehicle they use to try and separate you from your money, most unscrupulous business information/opportunity salespeople can be spotted with the help of the following checklist:

1. *A conscious attempt to create an image of opulence and enormous wealth.* They wear expensive clothing and ostentatious jewelry, and drive luxury cars. They show you a promotional video (or you see an infomercial) about a couple who worked long hours and were having trouble paying their bills until this wonderful new way to make money came along. They say that the word "job" is an acronym for "just over broke." The couple gives their testimonial leaning against a Rolls-Royce with a huge man-

sion in the background. Later in the video you may see them taking a luxury vacation, boarding a private jet or sailing on a huge yacht, which you are supposed to believe belongs to them.

2. *They wrap themselves in the flag and wear their religion on their shirtsleeves.* The implied message is "You can trust me (or this company) because I'm an American patriot who believes in free enterprise, and a deeply religious person who lives by the Bible." This means absolutely nothing. How do you know they're telling the truth? It's been my observation that genuinely religious and patriotic people show it by what they do, not by what they say. When someone starts telling you how patriotic and religious they are, get a death grip on your wallet and don't let go.

3. *A heavy emphasis on motivational materials, dreams and the power of believing.* Dreams, faith and motivation are important ingredients to any type of major success, but it takes more than that to be successful. You have to choose a career that matches your talents and passions, and put yourself in a position where the odds of success are in your favor. We can all walk on water if we know where the rocks are.

4. *Vague answers to specific questions.* When you ask, "What percentage of people make over $50,000 a year doing this?" you never get a straight or honest answer. Instead, the answer is something like "Anyone who really works at this business can get richer than they ever imagined." The truth is that if they published the true odds of success, very few people would buy what they're selling. Truly great

money-making opportunities almost never require much of a sales effort. A few people find out it's a great opportunity, the word quickly spreads and soon the world is beating down the doors. Do you think McDonald's has to knock on doors, lean on their friends, hold "opportunity meetings" or run TV infomercials to sell franchises?

5. *A concerted attempt to vilify and discredit anyone who suggests that the odds of success are poor.* Multilevel-marketing dropouts who quit after years of trying and losing thousands of dollars are sometimes labeled "losers." The implication is that they gave up too easily, and if they had just persisted long enough they would have made it big. The only problem is that you never get a specific answer on how much persistence it takes. Vocal dropouts are bad for business, so concerted efforts are made to discredit those who publicly share their experiences as a warning to others. Persons with websites who post stories of negative MLM experiences have been sued. In some cases, millions of dollars are at stake, and the company or one of its big distributors doesn't want any bad news being circulated.

6. *Buy, buy, buy.* There is always another book, tape, video or CD you need to buy or another motivational rally you need to attend in order to become successful in the business. There's nothing wrong with selling books, tapes and seminars, and I've made a good living doing it myself. But selling them under the pretense that they are necessary to be successful in a specific business where the odds of success are so poor seems horribly deceptive.

HOW TO PROTECT YOURSELF
FROM BEING TAKEN

According to an old racetrack axiom, "When a man with money meets a man with experience, the man with the money gets the experience and the man with the experience gets the money." One of the greatest benefits of education is the ability to learn from the experiences of others without having to endure the pain. You can protect yourself from being taken by following a few simple guidelines and using a little common sense. Think of the following recommendations as hurdles. Unless an offer clears all seven, don't buy it.

1. *Practice being a critical thinker.* Not a negative thinker, but a critical thinker. Critical thinkers don't react immediately to what they hear or see. They take time to reflect, ask for evidence to support claims and try to view anything that's presented in an objective light. Just because someone promises you the moon in person, in print, on TV or over the Internet doesn't make it so. Who is telling you this? What's in it for them? What hard evidence are they presenting that supports their claims? Do they have a hidden agenda? You can be sure that over 95% of the people who approach you with business and seminar opportunities do.

2. *Do your homework.* Call your local Better Business Bureau, state or county consumer-protection agency or state attorney general's office to see if you can find any information before spending your money. The Federal Trade Commission has an excellent website (www.ftc.gov) that provides up-to-date information on business and investment scams and what to look out for. Another excellent website is www.crimes_of_persuasion.com. A little investigation can spare you a lot of pain.

3. *Ask specific questions and get the answers in writing.* What's the refund policy if you aren't satisfied? What are the average and median amounts of money people earn after two years? Five years? Ten years? Ask to see specific evidence of earnings. If they don't provide you with specific answers in writing, walk away.

4. *Interview references provided by the promoter, but be very skeptical.* Very often references are just shills paid by the promoter to endorse extravagant claims. Skepticism is paramount, and a little paranoia can save you a bundle.

5. *Resist any pressure tactics to sign up today.* If the deal is good today, it will be good tomorrow. Pressure tactics and swindlers go hand in hand.

6. *Don't invest in anything that you don't understand.* Financial author and columnist Jane Bryant Quinn believes you shouldn't buy anything you can't explain to the average twelve-year-old. Understand what you're buying or walk away.

7. *If a business or investment opportunity clears all the previous hurdles, consider professional advice.* Pay an attorney, accountant or legitimate business adviser to look over any proposals, documents and contracts. As folksinger Pete Seeger once said, "Education is when you read the fine print. Experience is what you get if you don't."

If you practice being a critical thinker, most sales pitches won't get past the first hurdle. The old cliché is truer today than ever: "If it sounds too good to be true, it probably is."

FINDING GOOD LEGAL AND FINANCIAL ADVICE

If you have ever gone shopping for financial advice, you've likely been given several very nice brochures telling you how to find the right financial adviser. Well, you can throw most of them in the trash, because their true purpose is to convince you to buy investments and services from the company who gave them to you. Two excellent booklets that I do recommend reading are "The Vanguard Investment Planner" and "How to Select a

Financial Advisor," published by the Vanguard Group. You can order both free of charge at www.vanguard.com or 800-662-7447.

The field of financial planning is like the Old West—largely unregulated and crawling with snake-oil salesmen. Would you like to be a financial planner? If you answered yes, congratulations! All you have to do to become a financial planner is declare yourself one. Con artists, stockbrokers, insurance agents, accountants, trained financial planners, bankers and attorneys can all legally claim to be financial planners. I hope this disturbs you, because a little discomfort and caution today can save you a lot of money tomorrow.

The first step to getting good advice is to decide what kind you really need. If you want professional help, don't think for a minute that you're going to get out of paying for it. If you buy your investment products from an adviser, you're probably paying a steep price in fees and sales commissions for inferior advice. In reality, you're listening to a salesperson with a biased agenda. Bite the bullet and pay for recommendations from an objective and qualified expert who sells only his or her expertise. In the long run, you'll pay less and get better counsel. Bear in mind that this is precisely what over 90% of people don't do. It's a classic case of being penny-wise and pound-foolish. As a result, over 90% of all financial advisers are salespeople working on commissions.

Most people usually look for help in one or more of the following four areas:

1. *Comprehensive financial planning:* You may not need a financial planner and might be better off without one. In her excellent book *Making the Most of Your Money,* Jane Bryant Quinn writes:

> Most of us don't need professional planners. We don't even need a full-scale plan. To be your own guru, you need

only a list of objectives, a few simple financial products, realistic investment expectations, a time frame that gives your investments time to work out, and a well-tempered humbug detector, to keep you from falling for rascally sales pitches. Don't put off decisions for fear you're not making the best choice in every circumstance. Often there isn't a "best" choice. Any one of several will work.

In truth, you can learn the basics about financial planning by reading a good book or two on the topic or by surfing the Internet. Two valuable books are Quinn's *Making the Most of Your Money* and Eric Tyson's *Personal Finance for Dummies.* Websites such as Vanguard.com, Fidelity.com, Morningstar.com and scores of others can provide you with an enormous amount of solid, practical knowledge.

Assuming that you need a comprehensive financial planner, you want someone who will examine your assets, liabilities, insurance, taxes and spending patterns, and help you formulate a plan to achieve major financial goals such as buying a home, paying for your children's education and retirement. Ideally, you want a fee-only planner with a certified financial planner (CFP) designation. Here are several places you can inquire to find a planner in your area:

- **National Association of Personal Financial Advisors**
  www.napfa.org or 888-333-6659

NAPFA members are fee-only planners.

- **Cambridge Advisors**
  www.cambridgeadvisors.com or 888-834-6333

Fee-only advisors who focus on taxes and comprehensive planning for middle-income families.

- **American Institute of Certified Public Accountants**
  www.cpapfs.org or 888-999-9256

CPAs who specialize in financial planning. They may or may not be fee-only planners.

- The Financial Planning Association
  www.fpanet.org or 800-282-7526

The FPA will provide you with a list of CFP professionals in your area who may or may not be fee-only planners.

Based on the complexity of your financial situation, a good fee-only planner will likely charge you anywhere from $500 to several thousand dollars for a comprehensive plan. If you are considering a CFP in your area, be sure to verify their credentials on the Internet at www.cfpboard.org or call 888-237-6275. At the same time, you can see if they have any record of disciplinary action taken against them. You can be sure that there are at least several scoundrels working with bogus credentials.

Look for a financial planner who has clients with incomes, backgrounds and goals similar to yours. If you're a middle-income, conservative investor, an adviser who invests aggressively and has multimillionaire clients isn't a good fit for you.

2. *Tax preparation and planning:* If you have a simple financial life and you don't want to do it yourself, one of the national tax-preparation companies that come to life during tax season is probably adequate to prepare your income-tax returns. However, as your assets grow and your finances get more complicated, a good CPA is worth his or her weight in gold, especially if you own your own business.

3. *Estate planning:* Everyone needs a will. Without a will, the government decides who gets your possessions when you die. If the size of your estate is modest and your financial life is uncomplicated, have an attorney create a simple will. In addition to your will, have your attorney create a durable power of attorney and a living will. The power of attorney designates someone to act in your behalf if you become incapable of acting on your own. A living will tells health-care providers and others how you wish to be treated if you become seriously ill and cannot speak for yourself.

As your wealth grows into the multi-six-figure range, it's wise to consider the possibility of having a trust created. While they can be initially expensive, a trust can save your heirs a lot of time, money, and headaches when sorting out your estate after you're gone. Like tax planning, the laws of estate planning are complex, forever changing, and vary from state to state. In addition, there are various types of trusts and you need an expert who can decide which type, if any, would be beneficial for your estate. By the time you have need for a trust, you will likely have a good financial planner and/or CPA. Ask them to recommend a good estate-planning attorney.

4. *Investment advice:* If you invest your money passively, you don't need an investment adviser. If you want to consult with some helpful, knowledgeable people, go to the Vanguard Diehards forum at Morningstar.com. It's the best investment forum on the Internet, and the advice is free. You'll be amazed by who reads that forum and how much you will learn.

If you want to hire an investment adviser to help with your portfolio, here's the skinny on fees: *Low fees are good. High fees are bad.* This is one area where there is usually a clear inverse relationship between price and performance, because every dollar that goes into the adviser's pocket is a dollar less in yours. Your portfolio's asset allocation, fees and expenses determine long-term performance. Someone who wears expensive suits, works in a luxurious office, promises to outperform the market, invests your money for you and takes you to lunch doesn't determine long-run performance. He reduces it. It's okay to have someone hold your hand. Just realize that it's very expensive hand holding.

With any and all advisers, ask for references and check them out. Ask them how long they have been in business and ask how much their services will cost before giving the go-ahead.

If you hire fee-only advisers, you know how they get paid. If you don't, ask how they are being paid and how much, and get it in writing. It's your money, and you have a right to know.

If CPAs, attorneys or financial planners try to sell you investments or financial products, they probably have biased agendas that you don't want. At the very least, get a second opinion. Would you go to a doctor who gets paid a commission on medicine he/she prescribes?

Don't go to your friends for financial advice or referrals unless they are legitimately qualified, such as tax attorneys, CPAs or CFPs. Most friends won't know how to identify a good financial adviser. Odds are, they will recommend a friend who is a salesperson.

Learn as much as you can: your best protection is financial knowledge. Read books and financial websites, and participate in good online financial forums. You can blame a financial adviser for costing you a fortune, but it's still your fortune that's lost. As *Newsweek* columnist Meg Greenfield wrote, "There's nothing so dangerous for manipulators as people who think for themselves."

DO IT NOW
INSTEAD OF REGRETTING IT LATER

What you can do, or dream you can do, begin it; boldness has genius, power and magic in it.

—JOHANN WOLFGANG VON GOETHE

Creating the statue of *David* took a lot more than Michelangelo's know-how. It took his vision, time, talent, patience and, most of all, sustained effort. And that's precisely what it will take from you to reach your dream of financial freedom.

If you've read this far, you know what it takes to reach the winner's circle. But it takes much more than knowledge; it takes action. Knowledge is essential, but execution is everything. Winners know that financial freedom isn't won by what or whom you know. It's the product of what you do.

So when do you begin? *Today! Right now!* Every day you delay lessens the number of days you will enjoy financial freedom. Every day you delay means one more day you'll have to make a buck instead of enjoying it. Every day you delay lessens your odds of ever becoming financially independent.

Once you have the know-how, only two things can stop

you from reaching the winner's circle: death and your own behavior. The life of a millionaire is yours for the taking. All you have to do is be willing to do what it takes.

THREE EXCELLENT LESSONS FROM EARL NIGHTINGALE

Three of the best insights I ever heard on successful living came from the late Earl Nightingale. In his classic recording *The Strangest Secret,* he defines success as "the progressive realization of a worthy ideal." By that he meant that a person who sets worthy goals and continually works toward achieving them is a bona fide success. Even if he dies today, his life was successful because he pursued his own dreams on his own terms. Show me a person living his or her life that way and I'll show you a happy and fulfilled person. If you're planning and working toward financial freedom in a career of your choosing, you are already leading a very successful life. Getting to the winner's circle will just make it that much sweeter.

Earl's second insight was the one he dubbed "the strangest secret": We become what we think about. Life is largely a self-fulfilling prophecy, and your future will be the product of your expectations. So choose your thoughts carefully and focus on what you want rather than what you don't want. The way we think determines our decisions. Our decisions determine what we do. And what we do determines how successful we become. You are guided by your mind and will become what you think about most of the time. Focus on getting to the winner's circle, and your actions will draw you to it like a magnet.

Earl's third insight, although less well known, is my personal favorite: "Successful people don't get in their own way." We are quick to blame circumstances and others for our fate. Yet our lives are what we create with our choices. And that's why this choice is so important: You can choose now to do what it takes or live to regret it later. It's up to you. In the final analysis, life gives us reasons and results. Reasons don't count. As Christopher Parker remarked, "Procrastination is like a credit card: It's a lot of fun until you get the bill."

THE HIGH COST OF COMFORT AND DELAY

You want to have a wonderful life. You have dreams that you want to come true, goals to achieve, places you want to visit and people you want to meet. You want to be able to afford the nice things in life. You want the sum total of your life to be an incredible experience. And you want the financial freedom that will put you in control of your destiny and give you the time to enjoy and savor it all.

The key message I want you to learn is that all those things can be yours if you properly invest your time and money. It worked for me, it worked for millions of others and it can work for you, too. *But you have to make it happen.*

Staying in the time/money trap is far easier than climbing out. Just keep doing things the same old way, put off doing what you know needs to be done and you'll stay in your comfort zone. The two biggest obstacles to reaching the winner's circle are not other people and circumstances but poor habits and procrastination.

For example, most people foreclose their chances of ever reaching financial freedom because of the earning-to-spend habit. They get out of school, find a job, spend what they earn and carry a heavy credit-card debt, and those habits never change. There are always plenty of good reasons for not saving, which are usually rationalized like this:

Age 25: We're young and just starting out. We don't earn much yet and are entitled to have fun with what we earn. Besides, there's plenty of time.

Age 35: We have young children and high mortgage payments. Later on we will be earning more, the mortgage will be lower and the children will be grown. We can save and invest then.

Age 45: It's taking everything we earn to put the children through college. We had no idea how expensive it would be.

Age 55: We need to save more, but high-paying jobs and new careers are hard to find or begin at our age. Hopefully something good will come along and we can save and invest then.

Age 65: What are we going to save and invest with, Social Security? That hardly pays the bills. I just wish someone had told us about the importance of saving and investing when we were young.

Of course, someone probably did tell them, and they chose to ignore it. As political consultant James Carville put it, "You see those charts that say if you put away $500 a year starting at age twenty, by the time you're fifty you'd have a gazillion dollars. It just makes you ill that you didn't do it. You almost want to grab young people and shake 'em and say, 'Please don't make the same mistake I did. Please.' "

THE MAGIC IS IN THE DOING

I don't know how old you are, but I know that the clock is ticking and the winner's circle isn't going to come to you. Good things come to those who wait if they have a good plan and hammer away at it while waiting. Otherwise, you can forget it. According to a Chinese proverb, "A man must sit on a chair for a long time before a roast duck flies in."

Stories of people who achieve significant success usually have several common themes. First, they start with a dream that enables them to focus their resources on what they want to accomplish. Second, they begin where they are and go to work almost immediately to make it happen. It may take decades to see their ultimate dream come true, but that doesn't delay or deter them. They know that "someday" isn't a day of the week and waiting for the right time to start probably means waiting forever. Finally, they understand that commitment begets success. Once a person is committed to a course of action, all sorts of unforeseen happenings and opportunities seem to magically appear to help make dreams come true. It's like sailing. You put your boat in the water, chart your course, raise the sails and the winds appear. Your job is to harness the winds to carry you to your destination. As Goethe put it:

> Until one is committed, there is hesitancy, the chance to draw back, always ineffectiveness. . . . The moment one definitely commits oneself, then providence moves too. All sorts of things occur to help one that would never otherwise have occurred.

As you set sail on your journey to the winner's circle, use these pointers to get you under way and keep you moving in the right direction:

1. *Get out of your comfort zone.* Getting from wherever you are to the winner's circle starts on the day you decide to trade contentment for a commitment. Comfort and contentment are the archenemies of achievement, progress and personal growth.

As creatures of habit, we all get comfortable spending our time and money in familiar, predictable ways. Making progress toward the winner's circle requires new habits that are initially uncomfortable.

Once again, let's use saving money as an example, because lack of saving is the biggest obstacle to financial freedom. Bill has a good job and a paycheck mentality. He spends what he earns but realizes that financial freedom is rooted in saving. Some of his savings options are:

- To save an additional 1% of his salary each month. At the end of one year, Bill is putting away 12% of his pay.
- To moonlight, or to start a part-time business and save what he earns.
- To increase his earnings potential by getting additional education that qualifies him for a higher paying career and save the increase.
- To actively begin searching for a higher paying job or career and save any pay increase he gains.
- To take a similar job in a different part of the country where the cost of living is lower, and save the difference.

While Bill may choose any or all of these options, all of them will force him to change the way he spends his money and time. He needs to get out of his comfort zone, overcome fear, take risks and make significant changes. He also has to realize that new ventures, while not always successful, are rarely fatal.

Successful people know there is no free lunch. Commitment, work, risk, change and sacrifice are the price of success, but they're more than worth it. Getting to the winner's circle is difficult in the short run but infinitely easier in the long run. The most difficult kind of life belongs to those who forever owe their time and money to someone else.

The Comfort Zone

I used to have a Comfort Zone
Where I knew I could not fail.

The same four walls of busy work
Were really more like jail.
I longed so much to do the things
I'd never done before,
But I stayed inside my comfort zone,
And paced the same old floor.

I said it didn't matter,
That I wasn't doing much.
I said I didn't really care
For living well and such.
I claimed to be too busy,
With the things inside my zone,
But deep inside I longed for
Something special of my own.

I couldn't let my life go by,
Just watching others win.
I held my breath and stepped outside
To let the chance begin.
I took a step and with new strength
I'd never felt before,
I kissed my Comfort Zone good-bye
And closed and locked the door.

If you are in a Comfort Zone,
Afraid to venture out,

Remember that all winners were
At one time filled with doubt.
A step or two, and words of praise,
Can make your dreams come true.
Greet your future with a smile,
Success is there for you!

—Anonymous

2. *Be decisive and take action.* While it's important to think through important decisions, indecision is usually just another form of the greatest time waster of all—procrastination. Newton's First Law of Motion applies to people, too: A body in motion tends to remain in motion, and a body at rest tends to remain at rest. Choose a course of action, set some major goals and start moving. If you find yourself heading in the wrong direction, you can always change course.

Dream no small dreams. Do your goals scare you? If so, that's probably good. Courage is the ability to act when you are afraid. The people who try to go too far are the only ones who will ever know how far they can go. If you think a risk is worth it, go for it! You'll be amazed at what you accomplish over time with a concerted effort. The key is to do something every day, or almost every day, that moves you a step closer to the winner's circle.

3. *Rate yourself on the ten key choices.* Review the ten key choices for getting out of the time/money trap and rate yourself from one to ten on how well you are doing in each area.

LIFE CHOICES TO GET OUT OF THE TIME/MONEY TRAP

CHOICE	RATING
1. I'm living the life I want.	
2. I stack the odds in my favor.	
3. I'm a super saver.	
4. I'm improving the market value of my time.	
5. I do less better.	
6. I capitalize on the unexpected.	
7. I own the market.	
8. I am properly insured.	
9. I listen to those who know.	
10. I do it now.	

Pick several areas where improvement would be most helpful. Write some goals for improvement, put them on your to-do list and start working on them.

4. *Track, celebrate and reward your progress.* Put a financial chart on your wall or a spreadsheet on your computer where you can track your portfolio as it grows toward that ultimate goal of twenty times the amount of money you spend in a year. This will remind you to save when you're tempted to spend frivolously.

The journey to the winner's circle is a long one, so it must have the following key ingredients:

- You enjoy it.
- You stay focused on the ultimate goal.
- You keep motivated.

You enjoy the journey by choosing the right career. You stay focused and motivated by celebrating milestones of progress and rewarding yourself as you reach them. For example, if you enjoy traveling, you might celebrate every $10,000 portfolio increase with a weekend vacation, every $100,000 increase with a cruise and achieving a $1 million portfolio with a trip around the world. Just don't celebrate so much that it keeps you from getting to the winner's circle.

5. *Strive for excellence, not perfection.* Excellence is healthy, but perfectionism is a time killer. Spending an additional 90% of your time to get a 1% increase in performance is rarely worth it. An excellent idea put to work is far better than an unused one that's forever being perfected.

You won't be able to do everything perfectly, nor do you have to. Just keep doing your best and make daily progress toward that worthy ideal. Work hard in a career of your choosing and commit yourself to saving and investing toward the ultimate goal of financial freedom. Trust me on this: Those years will go by very quickly, and before you know it, your time and your money will be your own.

Now, put the book down, chart your course for the winner's circle and get started. If you have reached your financial goals or expect to in the near future, read on.

Part III

CELEBRATE AND ENJOY IT!

Shareholder: Now that you've become the richest man in America, have you established other goals?
Warren Buffett: Yes . . . to be the oldest man in America.

CONGRATULATIONS! YOU'VE REACHED THE WINNER'S CIRCLE, WHERE you can enjoy the harvest of your years of learning, working, saving and investing. You now have the freedom to spend your time any legal way you want.

At first it may seem like all of your problems are over, but I can assure you they aren't. Having an abundance of money and time puts you in control of your life, but it isn't going to automatically make you happy. Once you reach financial independence, doing the following four things can greatly enhance the quality of your life:

- *Stay* financially independent and out of the time/money trap.
- Make it a point to keep physically and mentally active.
- Experience the joy and personal satisfaction of giving back and making the world a better place.
- Finally, realize that the true joy of life lies in the journey and not some mythical destination.

Let's take a closer look at those four activities.

STAY FINANCIALLY INDEPENDENT

It is better to have a permanent income than to be fascinating.

—OSCAR WILDE

In my opinion, Sammy Davis, Jr., was the greatest entertainer of the twentieth century. He was a terrific singer, a marvelous actor, and an incredible dancer in his youth. In addition to all those talents, he did hilarious impersonations and could play every instrument in a band. He was truly a superstar. Just think of the tens of millions of dollars he must have earned in his lifetime. But when he passed away, the IRS seized his entire estate for back taxes owed. His widow was forced to move in with relatives.

Among celebrities, stories abound of great wealth followed by financial hard times. Here are just a few:

- Redd Foxx, the famous comedian and star of *Sanford and Son,* didn't leave enough money in his estate to bury him. Eddie Murphy paid his funeral bill.
- When Judy Garland tragically ended her life in 1969, her net worth was estimated at minus $4 million.

- Dr. Benjamin Spock earned royalties between $20 and $30 million (accounting for inflation) from his baby- and child-care books. Yet at the end of his life, his wife was writing friends and relatives for help to offset his $10,000 monthly medical bills.
- Derek Sanderson was the 1967–68 rookie of the year in the National Hockey League. He played for thirteen seasons, earned over $5 million and became one of the first athletes to make more than $1 million per year. By the early 1980s, he was broke and working at odd jobs at a country club for room and board.

It's one thing to reach the winner's circle and quite another to stay there. They both take work but of different types. Doing what it takes to stay financially free is Job One.

A MILLION BUYS FREEDOM, NOT EXTRAVAGANCE

In the 1950s *The Millionaire* was a very popular weekly television show. In this fictional drama, each show began with a very wealthy philanthropist giving $1 million tax-free to a very surprised everyday citizen. The story that unfolded was about what the recipient did with the money and how coming into such an enormous sum changed their lives. It was a great show at a time when a five-figure income was upper middle class, and $1 million was an inconceivable amount of money to all but the extremely wealthy. Today, a $10,000 annual income is well below the poverty level, and $1 million buys approximately what $135,000 bought in 1950.

Earning your first million is a wonderful achievement, but don't make the mistake of thinking that it entitles you to a life of expensive cars, yachts, airplanes, multiple homes and lavish vacations. If you do, you'll soon find yourself right back in the time/money trap. A $1 million portfolio will likely provide you with a sustainable yearly income of $50,000 before taxes, with annual cost-of-living adjustments. If you long for Robin Leach's "champagne wishes and caviar dreams," you'll need more than a million—much more. If you want a more lavish life of leisure, I have two words of advice: Keep working. But if you long to quit work and smell the roses, you probably can. Deciding how much money is enough is totally up to you.

Before you start depending on your portfolio for income, you need to create a financial strategy to make it last. That means answering two important questions:

1. How Do I Allocate My Portfolio?

My favorite strategy for allocating assets to provide lifetime income is similar to one recommended by Frank Armstrong, a Miami, Florida, fee-only, certified financial planner (www .investorsolutions.com). The plan is sheer simplicity:

1. You need two buckets of money: one for growth and one for safety.
2. Put seven years of income requirements in your safety bucket. Put your income requirements for the next year in a money-market fund and the remaining six years of the safety-bucket money in a short-term bond index fund.
3. Put the rest of your portfolio in stock index mutual funds. That's your growth bucket.
4. Arrange to have all dividends and interest from your funds transferred into your money-market account.

For example, if you have $1 million in investments, put $50,000 in a money-market fund, another $300,000 in a short-term bond fund, and the balance of $650,000 in stock index funds.

The safety bucket allows you to make withdrawals for seven years without having to sell your stocks in the event of a long-term bear market. Given that amount of time, the odds are great that any stock-market decline will rebound to new heights. As I mentioned earlier, while stocks go up and down, the only long-term trend is up. From 1950 to 2000, there were 12 bull markets that lasted 3.75 years and went up an average of 100%. During that same period, there were 11 bear markets that declined 25 to 30% and lasted an average of 9 months. As long as you can avoid selling your stock funds at depressed prices, you'll do fine. If you feel comfortable assuming more risk, your safety bucket can be as little as five years' worth of expenses, but no smaller. Don't put any money you will need in the next five years in the stock market.

2. How Much Can I Safely Withdraw from My Portfolio?

Plan to spend no more than 5% of your portfolio's value in a year. You may be thinking, "Why so little? If the stock market goes up an average of 11% a year, why can't I withdraw that?" It has to do with timing. If you began withdrawals in 1982, at the start of the greatest bull market in history, you could likely withdraw 11% and leave a substantial fortune. But if you began in 1969 and tried withdrawing that amount during the 1970s, when stocks were down, you probably would have run out of money before you ran out of time.

Average returns have nothing to do with what your actual returns will be when you're making withdrawals. You can drown in a river that has an average depth of one foot if you step in at the wrong place. Similarly, an overly optimistic withdrawal rate can pull you under if you are unfortunate enough to begin withdrawals at the beginning of a long bear market. With a five- to seven-year safety bucket and a 5% withdrawal rate, you won't have to rely on luck. If the market surges upward in your early years of leisure, you'll be that much richer.

At the end of the first year, and in every succeeding year, it will be time to replenish your money-market account and reallocate your portfolio. How you go about reallocating depends on how your stock and bond funds performed during the previous year. Here's the procedure for each of the four possible scenarios:

Case One: Stocks are up, bonds are up. Reduce the amount in bonds to six years of expenses (assuming you have a seven-year safety bucket). If any additional funds are needed to replenish the money-market account, sell stock funds.

Case Two: Stocks are up, bonds are down. Draw down initially from stock funds, but don't sell more than you made in profits the previous year. The cardinal rule of this strategy is never to sell stocks when they are down. If the money-market account isn't sufficiently replenished after selling stocks, draw down from the bond fund. Make a note to replenish the bond fund in the future when stocks are sufficiently up.

Case Three: Stocks are down, bonds are down. Draw down from the bond fund to the money-market fund. Once again, never sell stocks when they are down. You can replenish the safety bucket by selling stock funds when they go up, as they almost certainly will.

Case Four: Bonds are up, stocks are down. Draw down from the bond fund to the money-market fund.

While there are no ironclad guarantees, odds are that these allocation and withdrawal strategies will enable you to live out your life without going broke. Indeed, the odds are good that you'll accumulate a rather large fortune, enabling you to splurge some in your later years. While your ultimate goal may be to spend your last dollar on your last day, it just isn't a practical strategy. Better to die rich than to have a contest between drawing your final dollar and your final breath at the end of your life.

Yes, You Can Be Too Careful

When Jacob Leeder died in 1997 at age eighty-three, he left an estate valued at approximately $36 million. The enormity of his wealth came as a complete shock to Ann Holdorf, his friend of twenty-four years. Leeder never married, had no children or pets and lived in a modest one-story brick home outside of Baltimore. He drove a 1984 Oldsmobile station wagon.

Since he didn't have cable TV, he spent up to eight hours a day at Holdorf's house, watching stock-market reports. She ended up buying another set so she could watch her programs.

Most evenings Holdorf cooked dinner for Leeder at her home. Occasionally they would go out to eat at a cafeteria or a cheap restaurant. For her birthdays he gave her a check for $100. Whenever she would try to talk him into taking a nice vacation or dining at a fine restaurant, he would always say, "Not now, the market is bad." For her years of fidelity and companionship, Leeder left Holdorf just $150,000 plus a $100,000 trust fund. While most of his fortune went to taxes, the remainder was earmarked for two nieces, animal rights groups, and veterinary schools.

KEEP PHYSICALLY
AND MENTALLY ACTIVE

Happiness is like a butterfly. The more you chase it, the more it will elude you. But if you turn your attention to other things, it comes softly and sits on your shoulder.

—*AGING YOUNG* NEWSLETTER

Unless you're among the fortunate few, you spent decades learning, working, saving and investing toward the goal of financial freedom. Time was *the* scarce resource, and there was more than enough to do to keep you physically and mentally active. But once you reach the winner's circle, there's no shortage of time. Your calendar can be as full or as clear as you want it to be. Consider this: If you reach the winner's circle at age fifty, your life expectancy is thirty-three more years. That's longer than your working years. So what are you going to do with all that time?

Smell the roses. Take time to enjoy the harvest. The purpose of financial freedom is to allow you to create and enjoy the best years of your life. If you climb the mountain, you're entitled to enjoy the view. But don't just sit there and vegetate.

WARNING: RETIREMENT CAN BE
HAZARDOUS TO YOUR HEALTH

During the 1960s, an executive of a large corporation told me about a scenario that he had seen repeated many times where he worked. At that time the company had a mandatory retirement age of sixty-five. The scenario goes like this: An employee turns sixty-four and is eagerly anticipating retirement. He buys a calendar, puts it on the wall at work and strikes off the passing days of his last year of work. On his sixty-fifth birthday, the company gives him a watch, a plaque and a nice retirement party. He drives off into the sunset and a life of leisure. About a month later he comes to work one day to have lunch with his former colleagues, then visits a time or two after that. Six months later they attend his funeral.

Almost thirty years after hearing that scenario, I was in Australia, where I learned something very interesting from Jack Collis, a former insurance-company vice president. Jack is an excellent author, speaker and painter, a true renaissance man. When I asked him why he chose to write, speak and paint, he told me of two statistics he learned from actuaries while in the insurance business:

1. If you are over sixty and stay in a job you don't like, you have a 50% chance of dying within seven years.
2. If you are over sixty, leave a job you do like and do not replace it with an activity you like just as much, you have a 50% chance of dying within seven years.

These statistics contain a very important lesson: *If you want to lead a long and happy life, find something you like to do and keep doing it for as long as you live.* That's what Jack is doing. As I write this, he is in his late seventies and still going strong. He is writing a new book, making presentations and planning to hold an exhibition of his paintings.

According to Dr. Robert Butler, president of the International Longevity Center of New York, "Inactivity is one of the greatest threats to the physical and mental health of older people." Much of our physical and mental deterioration isn't due to aging but to inactivity and a lack of purpose. Any physical or mental ability tends to strengthen with practice and atrophy without use.

If you have a rocking chair, get rid of it. Life rewards those who physically and mentally challenge themselves with a much happier and longer life. Aging isn't a disease. It's a process. What we don't use we tend to lose.

REALLOCATING YOUR TIME PORTFOLIO

Reaching the winner's circle means taking a hard look at your time portfolio and possibly doing some serious reallocation. Without the constraints of a job and the need to earn a living, you're free to follow your bliss wherever it takes you. However, deciding how to invest your time can be difficult initially if your life has been structured for decades by a job or career. Once again, it's time to start dreaming and set lifetime goals. Here are some questions that might get your ideas flowing:

- What have you always wanted to know more about or study?
- Where have you always dreamed of living?
- What sports, hobbies or activities would you like to learn or become more proficient in?
- What places have you always wanted to visit?
- How can you share what you've learned that will benefit others?
- Is there another career or business you have always wanted to try?
- What cause(s) can you contribute to that would bring you the most personal fulfillment? (More about this in Job #3.)

Being financially independent doesn't eliminate the need to dream, to achieve and to grow. It just gives you more choices. Carry a notepad and a pen for a week or two and write down every idea that comes to your mind. Then pick out a few that you can pursue immediately. You'll be amazed at how quickly the days go by when they're filled with interesting activities. You'll wonder how you ever found the time for a day job.

As you decide how to allocate your time, keep these points in mind:

1. *You don't have to stop working.* If you still enjoy and get personal satisfaction from the work that made you financially free, there's no reason to give it up unless you want to. Perhaps you can scale back or pursue it on a part-time basis if you want more time for other activities.

While 75% of workers say they look forward to leaving their full-time jobs at some point, 90% plan to continue working. In addition, 70% say they would want to continue working even if they had no financial need to do so. That's very encouraging news when you consider that in 2030 there will be seventy million Americans over age sixty-five. That's too much talent and productivity to waste.

2. *Take a tip from the ancient Greeks.* Some years back, when I went to my doctor for a routine physical, he told me that the ancient Greeks believed we needed to do three things each day to stay healthy: exercise to cleanse the body; learn something new to cleanse the mind; listen to music to cleanse the soul. Add a fourth item to that list—laugh every day. A sense of humor is incredibly healthy.

Research studies are revealing that those who engage in regular physical exercise and challenging intellectual work throughout their lives significantly lower their risk of Alzheimer's disease. Get a regular exercise program that includes aerobic and weightlifting exercises. Cut back on the television viewing. Most of it is junk food for the mind and too passive to be mentally stimulating. Read good books or, better yet, write that book you've always wanted to write. Stay curious and interested. There's so much to learn. Who knows? You may actually become as smart as you thought you were when you were fifteen. As the late writer Mary Meek Atkeson remarked, "The best cosmetic in the world is an active mind that is always finding something new."

3. *Banish the word "retirement" from your vocabulary.* It's an artificial, out-of-date, twentieth-century concept. As long as you're alive, you have an innate need to feel like a useful, contributing, productive person. Never think of yourself as too old to do what you want to do. Youth may be wasted on the young, but retirement is wasted on the old.

4. *Learn from the centenarians.* Anybody who lives to be a hundred has to be doing something right. Clearly it helps to have good genes and to be a woman. Women centenarians outnumber men nine to one. While having the right genes may ultimately dictate who reaches the century mark, lifestyle plays a large role in how long and how well we live. A hundred years ago, only one person in five hundred lived to be a hundred. Today the Census Bureau is projecting that one in nine baby boomers (those born between 1946 and 1964) will survive into their late nineties, and one in twenty-six will live to a hundred.

Studies reveal that centenarians share a number of common characteristics in addition to good genes. First, they have a positive and resilient attitude. They remain emotionally stable, adaptable and flexible. They handle stress well, have a good sense of humor and accept things they cannot change. Psychological tests on centenarians at the Harvard Medical School revealed that every one tested low for extreme feelings of anger, fear, anxiety or sadness.

Second, they celebrate life and remain active participants. Centenarians aren't depressed about their age. They enjoy tackling new projects and learning new things; reading, writing and painting are common activities. Some live on the second or third floor of the buildings where they live, and climb the stairs every day. Because they stay physically and mentally active and involved with life, many of them have perfectly clear minds, and they appear far younger than one might think. According to the great philosopher and educator, Mortimer Adler, who lived to be ninety-eight, "Our minds, unlike our bodies, are able to grow and develop until death overtakes us."

Third, centenarians stay connected to other people. They have a network of friends and relatives they care about and who care about them. Like inactivity, loneliness shortens longevity. While centenarians like people, they also tend to be very independent and strong-willed and are used to having their own way.

Finally, many centenarians are spiritual people. They feel a connection to a higher power that gives them strength, purpose, guidance and sustenance. Not surprisingly, they come from all faiths.

In summary, keep moving and learning, and stay interested in the wonder of life. Enthusiastically tackle projects that you find enjoyable and exciting. Exercise, eat sensibly, stay upbeat and keep the faith. Surround yourself with positive people and avoid negative people like the plague. None of this will stop you from aging, but it sure will keep you from growing old.

EXPERIENCE THE JOY OF GIVING
SOMETHING BACK

In the quiet hours when we are alone and there is nobody to tell us what fine fellows we are, we come sometimes upon a moment in which we wonder, not how much money we are earning or how famous we have become, but what good we are doing.

—A. A. MILNE

Realizing that the end of his life is near, a man starts to worry about what will happen to his wealth after he's gone. He begins to pray, and God starts talking to him. He asks God if he can bring his possessions with him after death. God says no but offers a compromise: The man can bring one asset with him to heaven.

The next day the man starts loading gold bars into a bag to take with him. When he arrives in heaven, Paul gives him a strange look and asks what's in the bag. The man opens the bag, and the gold bars spill out onto the floor. He explains to Paul that God told him he could bring one asset with him to heaven. Paul looks at him and says, "Okay, but why did you bring pavement?"

The moral of the story is that what's valuable in one time and place isn't necessarily valuable in another. Similarly, you might encounter a day when your years of working, saving and investing provide a bounty of money and time far beyond what you and your family need to live out the rest of your lives in comfort and contentment. When that happens, consider donating some of your time and/or money to make the world a better place.

Americans are very generous people. Every year we collectively contribute over $150 billion to nonprofit organizations, roughly 85% of which is donated by individuals and families. Maybe you give regularly to your local United Way, place of worship, alma mater or any number of worthy causes. If so, you probably budget an amount, write the checks and send them off without much thought. That's great, and you're to be congratulated for it.

But once you reach the winner's circle, you can take your contributing to a level that may bring more personal satisfaction to your life than you've ever imagined. The key is to do it smartly and make it a win/win for you and the recipient. As the philosopher Aristotle said thousands of years ago, "To give away money is an easy matter and in any man's power. But to decide to whom to give it, and how large and when, and for what purpose and how, is neither in every man's power nor an easy matter."

To be an effective giver takes knowing yourself, investigating your options, planning, contributing and following up. Let's look at each of those steps.

FIND A CAUSE YOU CARE ABOUT

The most satisfying type of giving is proactive. Don't wait for a charity to come to you. Instead, find a cause that *you* care passionately about helping. Choose one or more that will bring you personal satisfaction from seeing your contributions make a positive difference.

Finding a good cause is like creating a profitable business—identify a need and fill it. Where your passions intersect with the world's needs is your cause; where you care most is where you are likely to do the most good.

Here's an exercise to help you discover your passions. Looking back on your life, what experiences brought you:

- The greatest joy?
- The most pain?
- The most hardship?
- The greatest opportunity?
- The most sorrow?
- The most success?
- The most love?
- The greatest sense of outrage and injustice?
- The greatest loss?
- The greatest faith?
- The greatest satisfaction?
- The greatest sense of accomplishment?
- The greatest improvement?
- The greatest change?
- The greatest happiness?

As you reflect on those experiences, answer a few more questions:

- What people or institutions do you credit for making your success possible?
- Who was there when you were in need?
- What should have been there when you really needed it?
- What did others do for you that you can pass on to help someone else?

As a young, poor boy, Andrew Carnegie spent hours reading in Colonel Anderson's private library. He never forgot the colonel's generosity that allowed him to learn. After becoming one of the world's richest men, he reflected on his childhood experience and committed over $60 million to establish a network of over three thousand municipal libraries throughout the U.S. He wanted every child to enjoy the benefits of free access to knowledge, and his gift is still giving over a century later.

Reflecting on the years of unconditional love and companionship provided by Maddie, his miniature schnauzer, PeopleSoft founder Dave Duffield created Maddie's Fund (www.maddies.org). The mission is to create a nation where no healthy dog or cat will be killed. The foundation intends to spend over $200 million to fulfill its mission through the creation of no-kill shelters, adoptions and aggressive spay and neuter programs.

In 1995, eighty-eight-year-old Oseola McCarty gained worldwide recognition when she donated $150,000 to the University of Southern Mississippi to provide scholarships for students in need of financial assistance. What made her donation remarkable was that she was a woman of extremely modest means who supported herself by doing other people's washing and ironing for seventy-five years. The donation was 60% of her life savings. About her gift Miss McCarty said, "I just want the scholarship to go to some child who needs it, to whoever is not able to help their children. I can't do everything, but I can do something to help somebody. And what I can do I will do. I wish I could do more."

Dave Thomas, the founder of Wendy's, was an orphan who was adopted in his youth by a loving family. In the hope of finding homes for orphans, he founded the Dave Thomas Foundation for Adoption in 1992.

Joan Kroc, widow of McDonald's founder Ray Kroc, fondly remembers him dressing as Santa at Christmastime and ringing the bell for the Salvation Army. The memory inspired her to donate $80 million to the Salvation Army.

All those examples illustrate how our experiences shape our passions. What would you like to be a part of: finding a cure for a disease that took the life of a friend or loved one? Providing assistance to abused women and children? Helping the homeless to become self-sufficient? The list is endless. After you list the causes you care about, target one or more to look into.

DO YOUR HOMEWORK

Once you've identified a cause, visit the various organizations you can contribute to and ask yourself—and them—these questions:

1. *Are the mission and values of the organization aligned with yours?* Be sure that you share the charity's vision for making a difference. Who do they serve? What needs do they address? Is it a local, national or international foundation? What makes them unique and deserving of your time and/or money? Are they fund-raising and performing services in a manner that you feel comfortable with?

2. *Is the organization established and fiscally responsible?* You don't want to give your money to a charity that may be here today and gone tomorrow. Look out for bogus charities with soundalike names where all, if not most, of the money goes straight into the fund-raisers' pockets. Some car-donation programs pay the towing service several thousand dollars and give just $100 to the charity. At least 70% of all monies collected by a charity should go to programs. Here are some sources for verifying charities:

- Philanthropic Research, Inc. (757-229-4631; www.guidestar.org) provides information on over 650,000 nonprofits. You can search for charities by subject area or location.

- Internal Revenue Service (800-829-1040; www.irs.gov) will verify that the organization has IRS approval if you plan to deduct your contribution.
- BBB Wise Giving Alliance (703-276-0100; www.give.org) checks charities for efficiency. Groups that spend over 35% of donations on fund-raising don't merit approval.

3. *Do the people and management of the organization possess the know-how to fulfill the mission?* Are the people knowledgeable, well trained, committed and capable, or do they impress you as well meaning but ineffective? You don't want to waste your time and money on good intentions.

4. *Are these people you would enjoy spending time with?* You need to know this if you plan to volunteer your time.

5. *Can you see where your money will go?* To take pleasure in donating, you have to see tangible results of where your money is going and the good that it's doing.

You should be able to get satisfactory answers to these and any other questions when investigating a potential charity. If you can't, consider taking your donation elsewhere. If no organization is addressing a need you see, consider starting your own foundation. They can be started with as little as $10,000.

TAKE TIME TO PLAN YOUR GIFT

Uncle Sam allows all kinds of tax breaks for those who give back, and you are entitled to make the most of them. Check with a tax attorney or a CPA before making a donation if you have any questions. How you make a donation can have enormous tax consequences.

For example, if you want to make a substantial donation, it's sometimes better to donate shares of stock or a mutual fund rather than cash. If the stock has appreciated, you don't have to pay the capital-gains taxes, and you get a full income-tax deduction for the contribution. The only restriction is that the amount of the donation cannot be more than 30% of your adjusted gross income. On the other hand, if the stock or mutual fund is worth less than you paid for it, it's better to sell the asset, get a tax deduction for the loss and donate the proceeds. If you donate cash, up to 50% of your adjusted gross income can be deducted.

If you are making a large gift, various types of trusts can be established that offer tax deductions and provide steady income to you or your heirs. Enlist the help of an estate-planning attorney in deciding if that's a viable option for you.

Giving can take many forms, and estate and tax planning are highly technical areas that you don't want to tackle alone. Whatever you do, don't write a check for a substantial sum before finding out the most cost-efficient way of doing it.

GIVE MONEY AND MOTIVATION

If you want your donation to make a difference, don't just write a check and be done with it. If you are giving a substantial sum of money to a charity or foundation, attach some strings. Promise to donate a certain amount if they can match that amount from new donors. Stipulate how your money will be used and get it in writing. Ask to see how your money is being spent. The purpose isn't to control the organization but to ensure that the donation goes for your intended purpose. Start by donating a limited amount and let them know that there might be a lot more where that came from if they make good use of your money. Being human, charities tend to get fat, dumb and happy when donors just hand over the cash and walk away. Give them an incentive to raise more money.

After you make a donation, follow up to see if your money is being invested effectively. You wouldn't dream of investing your money in a stock or bond fund and never check to see how it's doing. Take the same approach when you give back. Donating is just another form of investing, with the goal of increasing your personal satisfaction through making a positive difference.

In summary, getting the most from giving back draws on many of the same skills you developed to become financially free. You pursue what you feel passionate about. You set a few very well-focused goals. You invest your time and money in activities and organizations that will bring you the most satisfaction from seeing what you do make the world a better place. And you follow up to ensure that what you give back is making a meaningful difference. When you write the checks, you have the power to change things.

REMEMBER, THE JOURNEY IS THE JOY

Life is not to be endured but to be enjoyed.

—HUBERT H. HUMPHREY, VICE
PRESIDENT AND U.S. SENATOR

We have come full circle in our journey together. If you followed the steps in this book, you:

- Charted a life course
- Reached financial freedom
- Live your life on your own terms
- Manage your wealth prudently
- Remain active, vital and involved
- Continue to make the world a better place

In short, you've achieved some excellent and worthwhile goals. Yet it's important to remember that life is not a goal. It's a process to be savored and enjoyed every day.

Rather than explaining what I mean, I leave you with the words of two others who make the point with tremendous impact. When you finish reading their words you will more than understand the point I'm trying to make. You will *feel* it. The first is written by Ann Wells, a retired excutive secretary and freelance writer. The second is by the late Robert J. Hastings, a minister, editor and author of *The Tinyburg Tales*. Both essays are abridged.

A Story to Live By

My brother-in-law opened the bottom drawer of my sister's bureau and lifted out a tissue-wrapped package.

"This," he said, "is not a slip. This is lingerie."

He discarded the tissue and handed me the slip. It was exquisite; silk, handmade and trimmed with a cobweb of lace. The price tag with an astronomical figure on it was still attached.

"Jan bought this the first time we went to New York, at least eight or nine years ago. She never wore it. She was saving it for a special occasion. Well, I guess this is the occasion."

He took the slip from me and put it on the bed with the other clothes we were taking to the mortician. His hands lingered on the soft material for a moment, then he slammed the drawer shut and turned to me.

"Don't ever save anything for a special occasion. Every day you're alive is a special occasion."

I remembered those words through the funeral and the days that followed when I helped him and my niece attend to all the sad chores that follow an unexpected death. I thought about them on the plane returning to California from the Midwestern town where my sister's family lives. I thought about all the things that she hadn't seen or heard or done. I thought about the things that she had done without realizing that they were special.

I'm still thinking about his words, and they've changed my life. I'm reading more and dusting less. I'm sitting on the deck and admiring the view without fussing about the weeds in the garden. I'm spending more time with my family and friends and less time in committee meetings.

Whenever possible, life should be a pattern of experiences to savor, not endure. I'm trying to recognize those moments now and cherish them.

It's those little things left undone that would make me angry if I knew that my hours were limited. Angry because I put off seeing good friends whom I was going to get in touch with—someday. Angry because I hadn't written certain letters that I intended to write—one of these days. Angry and sorry that I didn't tell my husband and daughter often enough how much I truly love them.

I'm trying very hard not to put off, hold back, or save anything that would add laughter and luster to our lives.

And every morning when I open my eyes, I tell myself that this is a special occasion.

The Station

Tucked away in our subconscious minds is an idyllic vision in which we see ourselves on a long journey that spans an entire continent. We're traveling by train and from the windows we drink in the passing scenes of cars on nearby highways, of children waving at crossings, of cattle grazing in distant pastures, of smoke pouring from power plants, of row upon row of cotton and corn and wheat, of flatlands and valleys, of city skylines and village halls.

But uppermost in our minds is our final destination— for at a certain hour and on a given day, our train will finally pull into the station with bells ringing, flags waving, and bands playing. And once that day comes, so many wonderful dreams will come true. So restlessly, we pace the aisles and count the miles, peering ahead, waiting, waiting, waiting for the station.

"Yes, when we reach the station, that will be it!" we promise ourselves. "When we're eighteen . . . win that promotion . . . put the last kid through college . . . buy that 450SL Mercedes Benz . . . pay off the mortgage . . . have a nest egg for retirement."

From that day on we live happily ever after.

Sooner or later, however, we must realize there is no station in this life, no one earthly place to arrive at once and for all. The journey is the joy. The station is the illusion—it constantly outdistances us. Yesterday's a memory, tomorrow's a dream. Yesterday belongs to history, tomorrow belongs to God.

THE MILLIONAIRE IN YOU: SUMMARY

SEE IT!

1. Wealth is choice, not chance. If you really want to be financially independent, you will be. A financially independent person doesn't work for money. Their money works for them and brings in more than they spend.

2. Simplicity is the master key to wealth. The simplest rules for managing money and time are the most powerful. Remember LeBoeuf's Law: *Invest your time actively and your money passively*. The key to managing time is the 80/20 Rule. The key to accumulating wealth is the Rule of 72.

3. Think like a capitalist. Instead of earning to spend, resolve to build a nest egg of $1 million, or twenty times the amount of money you want to spend in a year.

4. Make the most of the twentieth century's greatest gift to you—an extra thirty years! If you are over twenty years of age, most of your future will probably be spent on the north side of fifty.

5. Remember that delayed gratification is not denied gratification. You'll get to enjoy the money when there's much, much more of it.

DO IT!

CHOOSE TO:	INSTEAD OF:
1. Live the life you want	1. The life others expect
2. Stack the odds in your favor	2. Against you
3. Be a super saver	3. A big spender
4. Increase the market value of your time	4. Working long hours
5. Do less better	5. Trying to do it all
6. Capitalize on the unexpected	6. Being derailed by it
7. Own the market	7. Trying to beat the market
8. Limit your losses	8. Letting bad luck ruin you
9. Listen to those who know	9. Those who sell
10. Do it now!	10. Regretting it later

CELEBRATE AND ENJOY IT!

1. Once you become financially independent, stay financially independent.

2. Stay vital and involved. Now is the time to do, see and experience all the things you didn't have time for in the past.

3. Experience the joy of giving something back.

4. Celebrate each day for what it is—a gift. That's why it's called "the present."

The bottom line: ***When you make smart choices about money and time, your life becomes a masterpiece.*** Share it with your children, your family and your friends.

ACKNOWLEDGMENTS

With special thanks to:

Richard Pine for many years of loyalty, friendship, encouragement, great ideas and guidance of my writing career.

My wonderful wife, Elke, who brightens my life with her love, companionship and support.

Ruth Mills, John Mahaney, Steve Ross, and Shana Wingert for their editorial assistance and publishing expertise.

John C. Bogle, the father of index investing, for enabling the average investor to invest with simplicity and at very low cost.

Neil Baum, Elke LeBoeuf, Taylor Larimore, Mel Lindauer and Neil Baum for reading selected chapters and providing great feedback.

All the Vanguard Diehards at the Morningstar.com website for their friendship, knowledge and help to so many. Bogleheads, you are the greatest!

INDEX

A.M. Best Company, 147
Action plans, 48, 49
Adler, Mortimer, 188
Alm, Richard, 68–69
American Association of Retired
    Persons, 71
American Humane Association, 61
American Institute of Certified Public
    Accountants, 160–61
Antman, Less, 134
Aquent, 57
Aristotle, 190
Armstrong, Frank, 179
Asset allocation, 14–15, 17, 130–33,
    135, 179–81
Astaire, Fred, 112, 113
Atkeson, Mary Meek, 187
Automobiles
    buying, 74–76
    insuring, 143–44

Bankruptcy, 117
Barbash, Fred, 66
Barber, Brad, 124
Beardstown Ladies, 120–21, 123
Beethoven, Ludwig van, 113
Bernstein, William, 128
Berra, Yogi, 15
Berry, Jim, 1

BEST criteria for goal-setting, 45–46
Bethlehem Steel, 22, 23
Better Business Bureau, 157
    Wise Giving Alliance, 194
Bogle, John C., 20, 128, 131
Bonds, 14, 130–32, 181
Brand, 88–89
Brinson, Gary, 130
Brokers, 15, 16
Buffet, Warren, 127, 175
Burns, George, 56
Burns, Scott, 65, 106
Business insurance policy, 144
Butler, Robert, 185

Cambridge Advisors, 160
Career choice, 56–57
Carnegie, Andrew, 192
Carter, Arnold "Nick," 41–44
Carville, James, 167
Census Bureau, 65, 67, 187
Centenarians, 187–88
Certified financial planner (CFP),
    160–61
Certified insurance counselor (CIC),
    148
Certified life underwriter (CLU), 148
Change, unexpected, 106–17
Charitable donations, 190–96

Charles Schwab Corporation, 131
Chartered property casualty under-
    writer (CPCU), 148
"Choice, Chance and Wealth
    Dispersion at Retirement" (Venti
    and Wise), 63
Christmas Carol, A (Dickens), 70
Clausewitz, Karl von, 19
Clements, Jonathan, 128
Clutter, 102
Coca-Cola, 107
Collis, Jack, 184
Comfort zone, 168–71
Compound interest, 24–28, 30, 32, 77,
    135
Conant, Lloyd, 41
Con artists, 152
Consumer Federation of America, 27,
    65
Copayment percentages, 142
Corporate restructuring, 94
Cost of living, 58
Cox, W. Michael, 68–69
Creativity, 89–90, 116
Credit-card debt, 75
Crises, 97, 103
Critical thinking, 157
Customer loyalty, 87

Daily goals, 23–24, 99
Dallas (television show), 70
David (Michelangelo), 1, 3, 41,
    164
Davidson, John, 72–73
Davis, Sammy, Jr., 177
Dawson, Brian, 46
Delayed gratification, 32–33, 201
Delegating, 101
Dial, Douglas, 128
Dickens, Charles, 70
Disability insurance, 138, 140–41
Discretionary time, 8–10
Disney, Walt, 113, 117
Di Teresa, Peter, 118
Divorce, 59
Do-it-yourself investors, 16
Domestic stocks, 14
Dot-com millionaires, 52
Downsizing, 86, 94

Dreams, translating into goals,
    44–50
Drucker, Peter, 93
Duffield, Dave, 192
Durable power of attorney, 161

Earthquake insurance, 138
Education, 55–56
80/20 Rule, 21–24, 96, 201
Einstein, Albert, 13, 24, 44, 113, 122
Eisenhower, Dwight, 97–98
Ellis, Charles, 124
Endowment, creating, 30–32
Estate planning, 161–62, 195
Estate tax, 67, 140
Evans, James, 79
Expectations, 39, 109

Farrell, Paul, 65
Federal Reserve System, 122
Federal Trade Commission, 157
Feedback, 90
Fidelity, 131
Financial planners, 15, 158–63
Financial Planning Association, The,
    161
Flood insurance, 138
Flynn, Errol, 71
Ford, Henry, 45
403(b) plans, 73
401(k) plans, 67, 73, 74, 133
Foxx, Redd, 177
Franklin, Benjamin, 10, 63, 85
Free-agent economy, 82–84, 95

Gardner, Jonathan, 4
Garland, Judy, 177
Goals
    daily, 23–24, 99
    lifetime, 48, 50, 93–94
    translating dreams into, 44–50
Goethe, Johann Wolfgang von, 164,
    168
Goodman, Ellen, 7
Grasshopper, 9
*Greatest Management Principle in the
    World, The* (LeBoeuf), 112
Greenfield, Meg, 163
Grizzard, Lewis, 59

Harris, Sidney, 92
Harvard University Center for Housing
    Studies, 59–60
Health insurance, 138, 141–42
Hill, Napoleon, 88
Hilton Generational Time Survey, 81
HMO (health maintenance organiza-
    tion), 142
HNW Digital, 4
Holdorf, Ann, 182
Holmes, Oliver Wendell, 12
Homeownership, 59–61
Homeowner's insurance, 143, 144
Hope Scale, 109
Houston, Julie, 116
"How to Select a Financial Advisor,"
    158
*How to Win Customers and Keep
    Them for Life* (LeBoeuf), 90, 112
Hugo, Victor, 99

Ibbotson Associates, 126
Immigrants, 53–55
Independent professionals, 57
Index funds, 14, 16–18, 120, 123–33
Inflation, 67
Infomercial gurus, 152–53
Insurance, 136–49
    automobile, 143–44
    business, 144
    disability, 138, 140–41
    health, 138, 141–42
    homeowner's and renter's, 143, 144
    life, 138, 139–40
    long-term care, 144–47
    personal liability, 144
    shopping for companies, prices and
        agents, 147–49
    three types of mistakes, 137–38
Internal Revenue Service, 152, 194
International stocks, 14, 132
Internet, 83, 85, 147, 160
Interruptions, 102–3
IRAs (Individual Retirement Accounts),
    26, 67, 73–74, 133
Isaac, Ted, 114–16

Jews, stereotypes of, 70
Job security, 82–83, 85

Job training, 85
Jordan, Michael, 112, 113

Keller, Helen, 52
Kendall, Donald, 51
Keogh plans, 73, 133
King, Martin Luther, Jr., 41
Kroc, Joan, 192–93
Kroc, Ray, 192

Lagniappe principle, 87–88
Larimore, Taylor, 133–34
Lateral loyalty, 89
Layoffs, 83, 85
Learning, 85–86
Leasing cars, 74
LeBoeuf's Law, 2, 5, 12–19, 36, 201
Lee, Ivy, 22–23
Leeder, Jacob, 182
Lehman Brothers Aggregate Bond
    Index, 132
Levi's, 107
Levitt, Arthur, Jr., 124, 150
Life choices, 55–62, 171–72
    career choice, 56–57
    education, 55–56
    health, 58
    homeownership, 59–61
    location, 58
    marriage, 58–59
    parenthood, 61
Life expectancy, 29, 32, 183, 201
Life insurance, 138, 139–40
Life Savers, 107
Lifetime goals, 48, 50, 93–94
Living wills, 161–62
Location, 58
Lombardi, Vince, 112, 113
Longevity, 29–30, 187–88
Long-Term Capital Management
    (LTCM), 121–23
Long-term care insurance, 144–47
Lottery, 27, 66
Lowenstein, Roger, 122
Lunch hour, working through, 80–81

Making the Most of Your Money
    (Quinn), 159–60
Malkiel, Burton, 125, 127

Mandino, Og, 117
Marriage, 58–59
Maximum lifetime benefit, 142
McCarty, Oseola, 192
Medicaid, 145
Medicare, 146
Mensa Investment Club, 121, 123
Michelangelo, 1, 3, 41, 111, 164
Microsoft, 103
Milne, A. A., 189
Money-market fund, 14, 132
Morningstar.com, 162
Mortgage payments, 58, 60, 77
Motivational speakers, 52
Mouton & Company, 30
MSCI EAFE (Morgan Stanley Capital
    International Europe, Australia,
    Far East Index)
Multilevel marketing (MLM), 153–54,
    156
Multitasking, 100–101
Mutual funds, 123–25
Myths of Rich & Poor (Cox and Alm),
    68–69

Napoleon Bonaparte, 12
National Association of Personal
    Financial Advisors, 160
National Center for Policy Analysis,
    68
National Endowment for Financial
    Education, 61
National Sleep Foundation, 80
Network marketing, 153–54, 156
Net worth, 8–10
Newton, Isaac, 171
Nightingale, Earl, 41–44, 165
Nightingale-Conant Corporation,
    41
Nordstrom, 82
Northwestern Mutual Life Insurance
    Company, 141

Odean, Terry, 124
Office Team, 80
One Door Closes, Another Door Opens
    (A. Pine), 114–16
Oswald, Andrew, 4
Owner, 9, 10

Parenthood, 61
Pareto, Vilfredo, 21–22
Pareto Principle (80/20 Rule), 21–24
Parker, Christopher, 166
Passive investing, 13–15, 18–19,
    123–35
Pay raises, 72
Perfectionism, 173
Persistence, 109, 117
Personal Finance for Dummies
    (Tyson), 160
Personal liability insurance, 144
Personal vision statement, 40–41
Peter, Laurence, 96
Philanthropic Research, Inc., 193–94
Physical fitness, 58, 186
Pine, Arthur, 113–16
Pine, Richard, 113
Platinum Questions, 90
Poor, in United States, 68–69
Positive attitude, 108
Post-it notes, 107
Prenuptial agreements, 59
Primerica, 27
Procrastination, 166, 171
Productivity, activity confused with,
    96–97
Property taxes, 58
Public Agenda, 64
Purcell, Patrick J., 67

Quinn, Jane Bryant, 127, 158–60

Renters, 59–60
Renter's insurance, 143, 144
Replacement cost, 143
Retirement, 184–86
Risk, 51–53, 55, 130–31
Rogers, Will, 78
Roosevelt, Franklin D., 52
Roth IRA, 26, 67, 73–74
Rule of 72, 21, 24–28, 30, 32, 77, 91,
    201

Safety bucket, 179–81
Salary Calculator, 58
Sales commissions, 123
Samuelson, Paul, 122–23, 126
Sanderson, Derek, 178

Saving, 63–78, 133, 168–69
Schwab, Charles (founder of Charles Schwab Corporation), 127
Schwab, Charles (president of Bethlehem Steel), 22–24, 99
Scudder Kemper Investments, 73
Sease, Douglas R., 128
Second chances, 110
Seeger, Pete, 158
Self-employment, 57
Seminar gurus, 152–53
SEP IRA, 73, 133
Sharpe, William F., 129
Side income, creating, 85–86
Siegel, Jeremy J., 129
Simon, Neil, 111
Simplicity, 20–23, 201
Sinquefield, Rex, 129
Slave, 8–9
Sleep, 80
Snyder, C. R. (Rick), 109
Spending log, 75–76
Spock, Benjamin, 178
Sport utility vehicles, 75
Stein, Ben, 70
Stengel, Casey, 123
Stereotypes, 70
Stevens, Sue, 144–45
Stock market, 119–33, 180, 181
Strangest Secret, The (Nightingale), 165
Success, fear of, 111
Support groups, 113
Swedroe, Larry E., 129

T. Rowe Price, 131
Taxes, 58, 67, 161, 194–95
Technological progress, 83, 95, 103
Term life insurance, 139
Thomas, Dave, 192
TIAA-CREF, 131
Time
    actively investing, 13–15, 19
    increasing market value of, 84–91
    management, 21–24, 92–105
Time and Wealth Grid, 8–11
Time log, 98–99
Time/money trap, 7–10, 15, 39, 82, 97
TIPS (Treasury inflation-protection securities) funds, 132

Tobias, Andrew, 127
Toll House cookies, 107
Trillion Dollar Bet (documentary), 122
Trusts, 162, 195
Tyson, Eric, 129, 160

Unexpected change, 106–17
Unique sales proposition (USP), 88–89
Universal life insurance, 139
University education, 56
Urgency, confused with importance, 97–98
USAA, 131

Vanguard Group, 131, 132, 158
"Vanguard Investment Planner, The," 158
Variable life insurance, 139
Venti, Stephen, 63
Visibility, creating, 88–89
VST (vision, strategies, tactics) approach to saving, 71–77

Wal-Mart, 82
Wealth accumulation, (see also Insurance; Life choices; Time)
    LeBoeuf's Law, 2, 5, 12–19, 36, 201
    passive investing, 13–15, 18–19, 123–35
    Rule of 72, 21, 24–28, 30, 32, 77, 91, 201
    saving, 63–78, 133, 168–69
When Genius Failed (Lowenstein), 122
Whole life insurance, 139
Wilde, Oscar, 4, 177
Wills, 161
Wilshire 5000 Index, 132
Windfall incomes, 72
Winfrey, Oprah, 37
Winner, 9, 10
Wise, David, 63
Women
    changing role of, 94
    investors, 124
Workaholics, 80
Working hours, 79–82

Zweig, Jason, 127

ABOUT THE AUTHOR

MICHAEL LEBOEUF'S mission is to help people find solid, practical ways to live and work smarter. He is an internationally published author, business consultant and a dynamic professional speaker and seminar leader. A former university professor, Dr. LeBoeuf taught in the business school at the University of New Orleans for twenty years, retiring as professor emeritus in 1989.

His previous books include *Working Smart, The Greatest Management Principle in the World* (also published under the title *Getting Results*), *How to Win Customers and Keep Them for Life* and *The Perfect Business*. The books have been published in over a dozen different languages, selected by major book clubs, excerpted in newspapers and magazines on all continents and adapted to produce sixteen different audio and video-cassette programs.

As a speaker, Dr. LeBoeuf addresses business and professional audiences worldwide. He has appeared on hundreds of radio and television shows, including *Good Morning America, Oprah* and *CBS Evening News*. As both a speaker and a writer, he possesses an ability to communicate with clarity and enthusiasm that make him a popular favorite. He lives with his wife, Elke, in Paradise Valley, Arizona. You can contact him via e-mail at mikelebuf@aol.com.